The greatest show on Earth

Welcome to our deep dive into the Masters and its Augusta National home

ONLY ONE GOLF TOURNAMENT greets you as a friend. The Masters holds iconic status in golf. Famous for its beautiful setting within an old horticultural nursery, Augusta National is renowned as the most beautiful golf course in the world. And whilst it is beautiful, it is also brilliant. It is a course that presents a thrilling test of golf, making the best players in the game earn its respect. Conquer it, and you are presented with a Green Jacket and a lifelong invitation to compete. For many, it does not get any better. This publication looks at the tournament's history, its most iconic moments and its holes, with exclusive input from tour players and legends of the game. If you love golf, you already love Augusta National. So this, my friends, is for you.

BRYCE RITCHIE
EDITOR

DC THOMSON

Speirs View, 50 High Craighall Road,
Craighall Business Park, Glasgow, G4 9UD
Tel 0141 353 2222
Email letters@bunkered.co.uk
Subscribe bunkered@dcthomson.co.uk
Online bunkered.co.uk
x.com/bunkeredgolf
facebook.com/bunkeredonline
youtube.com/bunkeredgolf
instagram.com/bunkeredgolfonline
threads.net/@bunkeredgolfonline

EDITORIAL
Editor Bryce Ritchie @BRitchieGolf
Deputy Editor Michael McEwan @MMcEwanGolf
Associate Editor Alex Perry @byAlexPerry
Gear Editor James Tait @jamestaitgolf
Performance Editor Lewis Fraser @lewisfras98
Content Producer Ben Parsons @_benparsons
Content Producer John Turnbull @JohnTurnbull03
Videographer Dexter McKeating @dexter.mckeating

SUBSCRIPTIONS
Subscription Enquiries 01382 575755
or bunkered@dcthomson.co.uk
Subscribe Online dcthomsonshop.co.uk/bunkered
or scan this QR code with your smartphone

ART & PRODUCTION
Production Manager Cheryl Gilbert
Designers Steve Curran, Jaclyn Bryson, Heather Rowan
Page Planners Hannah Renowden, Laura McLean

PHOTOGRAPHY Eve Conroy, DC Thomson
COVER Getty Images
PHOTOGRAPHS SUPPLIED Getty Images, Augusta National Golf Club, Adobe Stock, Fotolia.com, Press Association

Published in the UK by PSP Media Group Ltd © PSP Media Group Ltd (2024). Registered Office: PSP Media Group Ltd, Courier Buildings, 2 Albert Square, Dundee, Scotland, DD1 9QJ

Distributed by Frontline Ltd, Stuart House, St John's St, Peterborough, Cambridgeshire, PE1 5DD. Tel: +44 (0) 1733 555161 www.frontlinedistribution.co.uk. Export Distribution (excluding AU and NZ) by: Seymour Distribution Ltd, 2 East Poultry Avenue, London EC1A 9PT. Tel: +44 (0) 20 7429 4000 www.seymour.co.uk.
EU Representative Office: DC Thomson & Co Ltd c/o Findmypast Ireland, RBK House, Irishtown, Athlone, Co. Westmeath, N37 XP52, REPUBLIC OF IRELAND

bunkered is a member of IPSO (the Independent Press Standards Organisation) which regulates the UK's newspaper, magazine, and digital news industry. We abide by the Editors' Code of Practice and are committed to upholding the highest standards of journalism. If you think that we have not met those standards and want to make a complaint, please contact readerseditor@dcthomson.co.uk or bunkered, Speirs View, 50 High Craighall Road, Glasgow G4 9UD. If we are unable to resolve your complaint, or if you would like more information about IPSO or the Editors' Code, contact IPSO on 0300 123 2220 or visit www.ipso.co.uk

bunkered cannot accept any responsibility for any unsolicited manuscripts or transparencies. No part of this magazine may be reproduced without prior permission of the publisher. While every care has been taken to ensure accuracy, DC Thomson cannot accept any responsibility for any errors or omissions within the information provided. From time to time, telephone calls may be recorded for training purposes. ISSN 1363-6561

THE DEFINITIVE GUIDE TO THE
Masters
CONTENTS

WHAT IT'S LIKE TO PLAY AUGUSTA
Our man reflects on living every golfer's dream when he pegged it up on the golf course
Page 12

THE MASTERS THAT ROCKED THE WORLD
Jack's last win in 1986 and Tiger's first in 1997 – in their own words
Page 20

THE HISTORY OF THE GREEN JACKET
The fascinating backstory of sport's most famous item of clothing
Page 26

MY GRANDFATHER, BOBBY JONES
An exclusive interview with the great man's grandson
Page 46

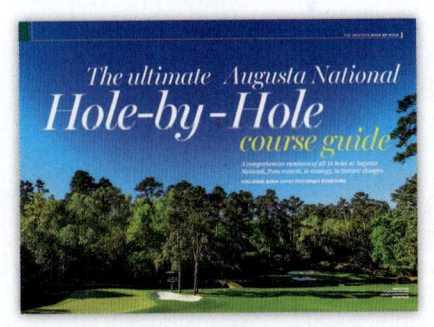

HOLE-BY-HOLE GUIDE
A full breakdown of the golf course, with stats, facts and historical info
Page 54

THE MASTERS IN BLACK & WHITE
Relive the tournament's early days with these rarely-seen pics
Page 84

THE SCOTTISH STARTERS
Introducing the two men who began The Masters' starter tradition
Page 106

THE TASTES OF AUGUSTA NATIONAL
From pimento cheese sandwiches to peach ice cream, we've sampled it all
Page 114

INSIDE THE MERCH SHOP
Where the tills never stop ringing throughout the whole of Masters week
Page 122

06 HOW THE MASTERS BEGAN // **42** THE GREATEST PLAYERS NEVER TO WIN
100 TRADITIONS UNLIKE ANY OTHER // **130** THE ULTIMATE MASTERS QUIZ

bunkered.co.uk

SHORT MEMORY
The par-3 16th has proved decisive in determining the outcome of many editions of The Masters but, to begin with, it was the seventh.

HOW THE MASTERS **BEGAN**

How the Masters began

The founding of the Masters marked a new era for golf. An era which has come to define the game's very best players. The major championship era.

WORDS **ALEX PERRY** PHOTOS **GETTY IMAGES**

FUN FACT: Augusta National was originally founded with the intention of hosting the US Open. That was certainly the wish of co-founders Clifford Roberts and Bobby Jones.

But with the USGA's flagship tournament scheduled for June, a month in which Georgia experiences mercury-busting high temperatures, the governing body politely declined the request.

Aside from hosting the very best in the game, Augusta was not planned as a club for locals, instead a spectacular golfing playground for the wealthy north-westerners who had, for decades, used Augusta and the surrounding areas as an escape from the bleak winters.

Indeed, it was with this in mind that the "National" was added to the club's name. And while other key components of the original layout – including a second 18-hole course and an on-site hotel – never

bunkered.co.uk > 7

made it to fruition, New York investment banker Roberts and Jones, one of the finest to have ever played the game, continued with their pursuit of instant nationwide recognition.

The Augusta National Invitation Tournament was born.

In its formative years, the event was not a success. Instead, there was little regard for a tournament held at a club struggling to survive.

Finances were such a concern that, to put up a prize for its new competition, the members were asked to chip in. The problem, though, was that there were only 76 of them.

Augusta, you see, had opened in January 1933, with the country still in the nadir of the Great Depression caused by the stock market crash four years earlier. This meant that not only was attracting cash-rich businessmen an issue, Georgia also found itself competing with Florida as a holiday destination. So when it came to hosting the inaugural Masters Tournament – as it would later be renamed – the club was handed $10,000 by the Augusta council with the intention that it would boost the city's profile to have some of the biggest names in golf playing in their backyard.

In return, there were promises of 20,000-plus crowds and an injection of more than $1 million into the local economy.

Unfortunately, for all parties, the numbers through the gates on each day barely topped four figures.

In the more linear context of the golf tournament, this didn't matter. Jones' attachment to the Invitational had attracted a strong field, and the huge $1,500 first prize will have certainly helped.

That year's US Open and PGA Championship, for contrast, came with a $1,000 top prize, while Open champion Henry Cotton pocketed just £100 at Royal St George's.

Jones himself also added to the intrigue. The career amateur had retired in 1930, having just won the calendar slam to take his tally of the game's four biggest trophies at the time to 13, to focus on the Augusta project. But he would dust off the clubs to play in his own tournament – and he continued to compete in a ceremonial role in 1948, though he never bettered his tie for 13th at the first attempt.

Alas, no amount of money or star power could get people through the gates. The council only offered up $5,000 for each of the second and third tournaments, and by 1937 had withdrawn funds altogether.

With a record low turnout the following year, the tournament's future was hanging by a thread.

A marketing plan that involved a rebrand to its current name and asking a local businessman to sell tickets to residents of Augusta helped

GOLDEN BELL
South African Bobby Locke putts out at the 12th in 1948.

HOW THE MASTERS **BEGAN**

BUILDING PARADISE
Bobby Jones, in front of his father, Bob, Clifford Roberts, and Dr Alister MacKenzie, hits a shot at the par-4 8th during construction in 1932.

OG MASTER
The first Augusta National Invitation Tournament champion, Horton Smith.

THE DOCTOR IS IN THE HOUSE

"Our overall aim at Augusta National is to provide a golf course of considerable natural beauty, enjoyable for the average golfer, and at the same time testing for the expert player striving to better par."

Co-founder Bobby Jones could not have called it better when he first set out to build a golf course on this pocket of land in Augusta's north-west suburbs.

Originally a plant nursery, the land was purchased by a hotel resort chain in 1925 that ran out of money before it even broke ground. Enter Jones, Clifford Roberts, and a group of investors with $70,000 in cash.

In order to bring Jones' vision to life, they turned to the legendary Dr Alister MacKenzie, who, in his native Yorkshire, had overseen the likes of Alwoodley and Moortown – the latter of which had, a few months prior, hosted the first Ryder Cup on this side of the Atlantic – as well globally-recognised layouts Cypress Point and Royal Melbourne.

But it was here, just a mile or so from the banks for the grand Savannah

River that separates Georgia and South Carolina, that would be MacKenzie's magnum opus.

The way that MacKenzie expertly routed Augusta National's now infamous 18 through the hills will be studied for generations of golf course architects to come. Indeed, no two holes are played in the same direction, while, apart from holes 10 and 11 and holes 17 and 18, each hole has a different par from the one that preceded it.

There is even a little nod to home, with the 15th at Augusta said to be based on the tenth at his original Alwoodley layout.

But it all ended sourly for Augusta National and MacKenzie.

The club's stark financial troubles were laid bare when it couldn't pay the doctor for his work, and the situation became so bad that, when MacKenzie was getting no response to letters, he eventually cut his $10,000 fee in half before writing to Roberts and Jones in distress.

"I am at the end of my tether, no-one has paid me a cent since last June, we have mortgaged everything. Can you possibly let me have $500 to keep us out of the poor house?"

It is thought MacKenzie received $2,000 – around $50,000 in today's money – before he died of a heart attack just months before the inaugural Masters.

MAJOR KING
It was Arnold Palmer who ultimately decided the Masters should hold major status.

HOW THE MASTERS BEGAN

somewhat, but it wasn't until 1966 that the tournament had its first sell-out.

By then, though, it was a major championship. And Jones and Clifford had Arnold Palmer, of all people, to thank...

MAJOR STATURE
It's strange to think there was a time when the word "major" wasn't used in a golfing context.

Bobby Jones, Gene Sarazen, Walter Hagen, Jim Barnes, the Tom Morrises. All legends of the game we retrospectively consider multiple major champions. But it wasn't the case back then.

There was a period in history when the Open Championship, US Open, Amateur Championship and US Amateur were considered the most prestigious tournaments in the game.

Only Jones managed to win all four, including that run in 1930 that saw him put all four trophies in his cabinet.

But with the rise of the professional game in the 1940s and '50s, the term "major" eventually came to describe the Masters, US Open, The Open, and PGA Championship.

And it was all down to Arnold Palmer's winning mentality.

Following his Masters and US Open victories to open the 1960 season, The King declared he would be chasing "a grand slam of my own" to rival Jones' achievement from 30 years prior.

According to his autobiography, *A Golfer's Life*, it was on a trans-Atlantic flight to Ireland for that summer's Canada Cup ahead of The Open at St Andrews when Palmer and friend Bob Drum, a journalist with the *Pittsburgh Press*, decided to start making his dream a reality.

Until then, the Western Open and the North & South Open were generally thought of by Americans as two of the big four, while the British PGA Match Play Championship commanded the same respect on this side of the Atlantic.

But what would join The Open and US Open in this quartet of most sought-after titles?

The PGA Championship, an annual tournament between the members of the Professional Golfers' Association of America, was an obvious choice, but it was the fourth that proved more difficult.

In the end, as it so often does, it came down to money.

The Masters, at the time, offered the biggest first prize in the game. Indeed, Palmer had just won $17,500 for his win at Augusta, while the US Open banked him just north of $14,000.

And so the Grand Slam, and the golf's major championship era, was born.

"One thing led to another," Palmer wrote. "Drum got the British press all excited about it and everybody picked up on it at St Andrews that year."

And while Palmer fell one short on his Open debut that year, he would ultimately do the same in his own Grand Slam ambitions.

To this day only Sarazen, Ben Hogan, Gary Player, Jack Nicklaus and Tiger Woods have joined this ultra-exclusive club.

But, like Jones and the Masters, its creator failed to gain membership.

> **Choosing a fourth major proved to be difficult. But in the end, it came down to money. And so the Grand Slam, and golf's major championship era, was born.**

bunkered.co.uk › 11

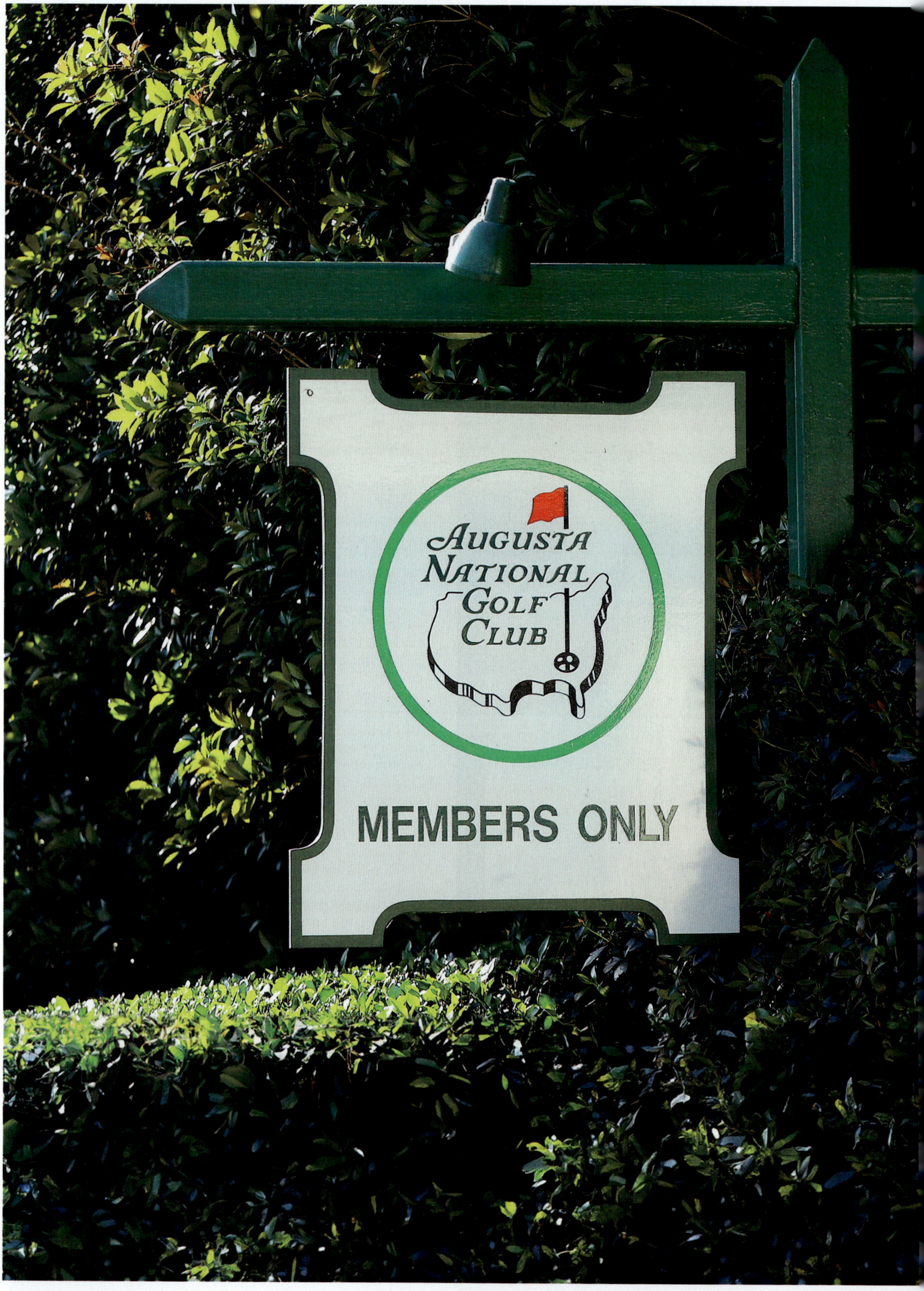
AUGUSTA
NATIONAL
GOLF
CLUB
MEMBERS ONLY

PLAYING **AUGUSTA**

THE MONDAY FINISH

'Let me tell you about the time I played Augusta'

A matter of hours after Jon Rahm won the 2023 Masters, bunkered's Michael McEwan lived every golfer's dream when he pegged it up at Augusta National. This is how it went…

PHOTOS **GETTY IMAGES**

THERE ARE FEW things as tedious as hearing about somebody else's round of golf. Having said that, perhaps you will indulge me this once because, whilst all men are created equal, all rounds are not. On April 10, 2023, I was lucky enough to fulfil a lifelong ambition. I played Augusta National. As an accredited member of the media covering the Masters, I was invited to enter the annual media lottery, from which 28 lucky souls are drawn and allowed to peg it up on the iconic course the morning after the latest Green Jacket recipient is decided.

IT IS, IN ITS OWN WAY, a tradition unlike any other. Dating back many years, the 'Monday Golf Outing', to give it its official name, is Augusta National's way of thanking media for covering the Masters. Contrary to what some wizened hacks would have you believe, the Green Jackets do value the coverage they get. It's not for nothing that they shelled out a reported $50 million on a new, permanent media centre at the bottom of the driving range in 2017.

This was my third visit to the Masters. I was there in 2019 when Tiger Woods won his fifth title and, after Covid scuppered return visits in 2020 and 2021, I was back to see Scottie Scheffler win his first major in 2022. Both times, I entered the media lottery. Both times, no dice.

But 2023 was different. Let's call it third time lucky.

It's easy to say this after the fact but I had a strong feeling this was going to be my year. For example, on Wednesday afternoon, I ventured out of the media centre and popped down to the merch shop. Monday and Tuesday are intensely busy, but Wednesday is typically quieter, so, as the Par-3 Tournament was getting under way, I took the chance to duck out. After I'd emptied my bank account into one of the tills, I found myself next to the big leaderboard adjacent to the first fairway and considering going for a walk around the course.

Because most people are watching the cutesy chaos Par-3, the 'main' course tends to be quite quiet, so this is the perfect chance to see it. The strangest feeling came over me, though. "Don't worry about it," said a voice in my head. "You'll get to see it all on Monday." And so I went back to the media centre. It's hard to explain but I almost expected to be drawn.

I was on FaceTime with my wife and daughter back home in Scotland when I found out. We were talking about my parents' upcoming golden wedding anniversary when I glanced to my left and spotted the television screen behind the reception desk. It was displaying the names of the media who had been successful in the lottery. The last name on show: Michael McEwan.

"Holy f***!" I blurted out.

"What's happened?" asked my wife, instantly panicked.

I replied: "I'm playing the golf course on Monday!"

We spoke for a few more minutes but I can't remember a word of it. My mind was mush. After we hung up, I checked and re-checked the screen. Sure enough, it was happening.

My next call was to *bunkered* editor Bryce Ritchie.

"What's happening?" he asked.

"Never mind what's happening today," I grinned. "Ask me about what's happening on Monday?"

He twigged immediately. Bryce has been to the Masters three times. He knows the deal.

"No. F***ing. Way," he replied. "Are you serious?"

"Deadly."

"You're playing Augusta National?"

"I'm playing Augusta National."

There was nothing either of us could do but laugh. We've worked together for 20 years. Before we started going to the Masters, we watched it in each other's homes. The idea that one of us was getting to actually play the course was surreal.

14 ‹ bunkered.co.uk

PLAYING AUGUSTA

"I'm not even jealous," he lied. "Honestly, that's amazing."

My next call was to my mum and dad. I'm the youngest of four and we're not a particularly sporty family. That said, there were always a handful of events that I vividly remember being on TV growing up. The London Marathon is one. Wimbledon another. So, too, the Masters.

I have a particularly strong memory of the 1996 tournament. It was shortly before we swapped our home in the Orkney Islands for Glasgow. I can still picture dad beckoning me over to watch the action. Despite not being a golfer, he has always loved the Masters because of Augusta National ("Look at those azaleas!") and Seve Ballesteros ("A genius!"). That year, he was insistent I watch it with him because there was a young guy "with a funny name" who's "going to be a huge deal". Tiger Woods, obviously.

The Masters was my introduction to golf. Had it not been for my parents watching it and encouraging me to pay attention to it, there's a good chance I wouldn't be writing this. So, to tell them I was going to get to play the course was special.

I was basking in the well wishes of several fellow journos – and, thanks to Bryce breaking the news on social media, countless people on Twitter – when the trees fell near the 17th tee and Friday's play was suspended.

I immediately started doing all kinds of mental gymnastics. Half the field had still to finish their second round and the forecast for Saturday was grim. Very, very grim. Several inches of rain was expected to fall overnight, with downpours continuing throughout the day. I even overheard two English reporters discussing the prospect of Saturday being completely washed out.

Sod the tournament, what did that mean for *my* round? If it went to a Monday finish, would my invitation roll into Tuesday instead? Alternatively, would they just carry the round over to next year?

I'd get my answer at a Sunday morning briefing for all lottery winners. In the meantime, all I could do was watch and wait.

ICONIC
The view from the tee on the famous par-3 12th. Many players have seen their Masters hopes dashed here over the years.

bunkered.co.uk › 15

My gut – and several fellow reporters – told me it was Monday or bust. And that made for an uncomfortable weekend.

By Saturday lunchtime, I was feeling good again. A combination of the weather not being quite as bad as forecast and Augusta National's investment in SubAir technology meant the course was holding up well against the conditions. Things appeared to be back on track.

Then came my next problem: I had a tee time but no clubs. I'm not an especially superstitious person but taking my clubs to Augusta felt like a sure way to jinx my prospects. I'd worry about clubs if and when my name got pulled. Ewan Murray, the golf correspondent for *The Guardian*, found himself in the same position a few years earlier and had managed to rent a cobbled-together set from a nearby second-hand golf shop. "You go in, explain the situation to them, and they'll give you a bag to fill up," he told me. "Dead easy."

Around lunchtime on Saturday, I jumped in my rental car and went to the shop he'd recommended. By this point, the rain had gone from steady to torrential. I went in and explained the situation to an elderly gent behind the counter.

He fixed me a quizzical look. "I don't think we do that no more," he drawled. "Let me go check."

As he shuffled out of view, I heard the unmistakable sound of an air horn coming through the speakers of the TV hanging from the ceiling. I glanced up. Play suspended. As Jim Nantz uttered the words "no more golf today", I knew my chances of playing were slipping away.

At that point, the old guy returned. "Just as I thought, we stopped doing that a couple years ago," he said. Pointing to the TV, he added: "Don't think it'll matter anyway. They're still gon' be playin' on Monday."

All at once, my heart sank and broke, and I trudged back to my car. I sat behind the wheel for about five minutes just staring at the rain. I took every splash of rain on the windscreen personally. It sounds ridiculous but I was, in part, dreading the inevitable influx of schadenfreude. I even started to mentally compose the first few paragraphs of a "How my Augusta dream turned into a nightmare" piece.

The last Monday finish at Augusta occurred ten months before I was born, so the prospect of such a delay in the year I got picked to play the course felt as inevitable as it did cruel.

Driving back to my motel, I tried to do the math. The leaders still had 11 holes of their third round to complete. To finish on time, they'd need to play 29 holes on Sunday. Not out of the question. There just wouldn't be a huge amount of wiggle room. Assuming Mother Nature co-operated – and the forecast suggested she would – there was probably enough daylight for three holes of a playoff if required. Tight, but doable.

On Sunday morning, we had our meeting with Augusta officials, where we were given a list of dos and don'ts for our round. The

FIRST IMPRESSIONS
The view from the middle of the first fairway. You ideally want to be a little more left of this position to open up the green.

PLAYING **AUGUSTA**

prospect of a Monday finish came up. "If that happens," we were told, "then unfortunately you won't be playing."

Worried glances were exchanged. Nobody said it out loud, but everyone was thinking the same thing.

By lunchtime, things looked gravy again. The third round had been completed and the leaders were scheduled to go out in pairs – another good sign – at their customary time (between 2.30pm and 3pm).

I still didn't have any clubs, though. I called Augusta Country Club. No dice. I asked a few colleagues. No dice. Finally, I called the River Golf Club in North Augusta, where I spoke to head pro Wayne Ackerman.

Once again, I explained my predicament. "I'll be honest," I said. "I'm starting to run out of options. Please tell me you can help."

"Sure thing," said Wayne.

"If you got money, we got clubs."

Five minutes later, I was in the car. I figured I wouldn't be the only lottery winner phoning him.

Clubs secured, I drove back to the media centre to enjoy the rest of the round. As Rahm and Koepka in the final group stood on the third tee, I glanced at my watch. Forty-five minutes to play two holes? Uh-oh! At this rate, there would be no time for a playoff.

Over the next four hours, I became irrationally obsessed by Patrick Cantlay and his glacial behaviour. I'd beaten the odds by being drawn in the lottery in the first place and, for good measure, had seen off falling trees and rain delays only to be defeated by a multi-millionaire human traffic jam who moves with the urgency of a three-legged turtle? It felt like the universe was taking the piss.

It wasn't until Rahm removed his baseball cap

bunkered.co.uk › 17

as he approached the 18th green that I relaxed. I checked the weather forecast for the millionth time in 48 hours. All good.

Game on.

AS DAWN BROKE ON MONDAY, I was already wide awake. Notwithstanding my 11.20am tee time, I had to pack my bags because I was driving straight to the airport in Atlanta when I finished up later that afternoon. Time was of the essence.

Per club rules, you're not allowed to arrive more than one hour before your tee time. Any earlier and they'll turn you away.

Having checked out, I drove to Washington Road. I wanted to be close in case of any traffic jams or hold-ups.

One of the best bits of advice I got was to have breakfast before arriving. With only 60 minutes to look around the clubhouse, get changed, go to the pro shop (this is where they sell the mega-exclusive Augusta National-branded merch) and hit shots, you don't want to be wasting any time on eating. So, at 9.45am, I was in the Waffle House, dressed for golf and scoffing my budget brekkie.

At precisely 10.20am, I turned right onto Magnolia Lane where a sheriff's officer waved me down.

"Good morning, sir," he drawled. "Can I see your documents?"

I showed him my invite.

"Okay, 11.20am," he said, studying the card. "Right on time."

As if I was going to be late!

As he handed it back, the steel bollards lowered in unison.

"Just drive up to the clubhouse and they'll take care of you," he added. "Have a great day."

The drive up Magnolia Lane has been filmed and shared on social media countless times before. We all know what it looks like by now. Even so, it's surreal. A couple of things: one, it's a lot longer it looks; two, it's infinitely cooler than you can imagine. All I could do was giggle to myself.

As I drove around Founder's Circle and pulled up at the front door, a caddie opened the back door of the car and took away my clubs and a valet grabbed the keys. Suddenly, I was in the clubhouse. It's a small, simple building with not so much as a thread out of place. It's like a show home. Off to the right as you enter, there's a spiral staircase that leads to the Champions' Locker Room. Ordinarily the preserve of Green Jacket owners, this space is used by media lottery winners, each of whom is randomly assigned a locker. Moving through the room, no bigger than three-quarters the size of one half of a tennis court, I scanned the lockers looking for my name.

Suddenly, there it was: "Michael McEwan". A brass plaque above my name showed which former Masters champion the locker was reserved for.

Seve Ballesteros.

I'm not ashamed to admit I welled up. Seve, the first European to win the Masters, my dad's favourite golfer and me, born in 1984 – and we all know what he did at St Andrews that year – getting to "share" a space with him? It was too much.

After spending far too much in the pro shop, I went to the range where my caddie – clad in the white overalls – was standing next to my bag. I really lucked out. Me and Glen, or "No Pin Glen" as his fellow loopers call him (apparently, he's a bit shy at tending the flag!), hit it off immediately. He reckons he's caddied more than a thousand rounds at Augusta National.

"Does it ever get old?" I asked him.

"Never."

Now, a confession: I hadn't hit a ball in 2023 prior to rocking up at Augusta. Genuinely. The first shot I hit was a fat wedge on the range. The next was far better. I then hit two 7-irons (beautifully, I might add) and that was it. Off to the first tee.

That's where I met my playing partners: a Chinese reporter called Xieng Jiu; Alex Trautwig, a photographer with Getty Images; and Bob Casper. Bob is the long-standing host of Real Golf Radio. He also happens to be the son of the 1970 Masters champion, Billy Casper.

Apart from a few Augusta National officials, there was nobody else near the tee. After Bob ripped a drive down the middle, it was my turn to go. A lot of people have asked me how nervous I felt. The honest answer is not particularly. Sure, there were some butterflies, but nothing compared to, say, the Old Course. Missing the world's widest fairway, invariably with a lot of people watching, is not something anybody wants to be known for. I've played St Andrews three times, and, on every occasion, I've been extremely nervous. Augusta National brings its own pressure but the first on the Old Course is world-renowned, which Augusta's isn't.

More than anything, I was just excited to get going. It sounds mega cheesy but as I stood behind my ball and looked down the fairway, I was thinking of my little girl and how cool it will be to tell her about all this when she's old enough to understand.

As luck would have it – and it was luck – I hit a perfect drive; a lovely little cut that came to rest in the middle of the fairway just beyond the bunker. I even got a round of applause from the assembled officials. Rory McIlroy would have paid good money for that shot on Sunday in 2018.

I won't bore you with a full blow-by-blow account of my round. Instead, here are a few highlights and observations.

First of all, yes, it's hilly. Much hillier than it looks on TV and, in a strange way, much hillier than it looks from the other side of the ropes.

Secondly, we were playing from the members' tees. All told, it comes in at 6,350 yards, not the 7,545 yards players competing in the Masters must wrestle with. We did, though, have Sunday

> **All at once, my heart sank and broke. I even started to mentally compose the first few paragraphs of a 'How my Augusta dream turned into a nightmare' piece.**

PLAYING **AUGUSTA**

AMEN!
Looking back down the 13th hole towards the tee and 12th green, the scene of so much Masters drama down the years.

pins to contend with.

The greens? Stupendously good and stupendously tough. On the first, I chipped on from off the right-hand side of the dance floor and, at first glance, I thought I had absolutely nailed it. I ended up off the front edge. "Welcome to Augusta," said one of the other caddies with a knowing chuckle. On the fifth, I was about 25 feet from the flag and my caddie asked me to tell him what I saw. I had it around 60% weight and a little right to left. Turns out it was 110% weight and left to right. Because of the grain, some downhill putts felt slow, whilst some uphill putts seemed fast. Fast, slick and harder to read than Finnegans Wake, they are, hands down, the best greens I have ever putted on, all of which makes it remarkable that I had zero four-putts and only one three-putt, on the 16th, frustratingly.

There's no doubt that the back nine is where most of the fun is to be found. Ten is fantastic fun – if you hit it in the right spot off the tee – whilst 11 is a simply brilliant hole. It was a lot different from how I'd pictured it in my mind's eye. Not off the tee so much, but when you get up to the crest of the hill. The green is suddenly right there and, Holy Fuzzy Zoeller, it's intimidatingly small. I made an exceptional five there after my one and only shank of the day from the middle of the fairway and a flubbed chip from next to the 12th tee.

And so to 12. Golden Bell. Arguably the most famous par-3 in the world.

What can I tell you? For one thing, it's beautiful. For another, it's terrifying. As you stand on the tee, you can't help but think of all the would-be Masters champs whose hopes have been dashed by it. Jordan Spieth in 2016; Tony Finau, Francesco Molinari and Brooks Koepka in 2019. As I waited my turn, the words of Jack Nicklaus echoed in my mind. "It's the hardest tournament hole in golf." Thanks, Jack.

In the end, I hammered a 7-iron right over the top of the flag. It ended up being a little big but the sight of the ball in mid-air, sailing on that aggressive a line, knowing I'd (a) not shanked it and (b) cleared the creek was extremely satisfying. I made bogey but that was six better than Tiger managed on the final day in 2020, so I'll take it.

Fourteen was a pleasant surprise. I'd always thought of it as being a bit like an ad break in the middle of an amazing movie. So wrong. It's a seriously underrated hole.

Finally, eighteen. I'd promised myself that, irrespective of where my drive went, I'd throw my ball in the fairway bunker to try to recreate Sandy Lyle's iconic shot in 1988. Particularly with that year having been his final Masters appearance, it felt only right. I rattled a 7-iron into the right greenside bunker.

A couple of putts later, it was over. With a few asterisks, I shot a 97. All things considered, I'm more than happy with that. Everybody shook hands, and, within ten minutes, I was back in the car and homeward-bound.

I'm now barred from entering the media lottery for the next seven years but, honestly, I don't think I'll ever re-enter. What's the point? I got to live a dream and it completely exceeded my expectations. How could a second, or a third, or a fourth go possibly be better?

Amongst the many tweets I received, one stood out. "Today you will live the dream on behalf of us all," it read. "Breathe deep, walk tall and smell the azaleas. Enjoy every moment."

I absolutely did.

bunkered.co.uk > 19

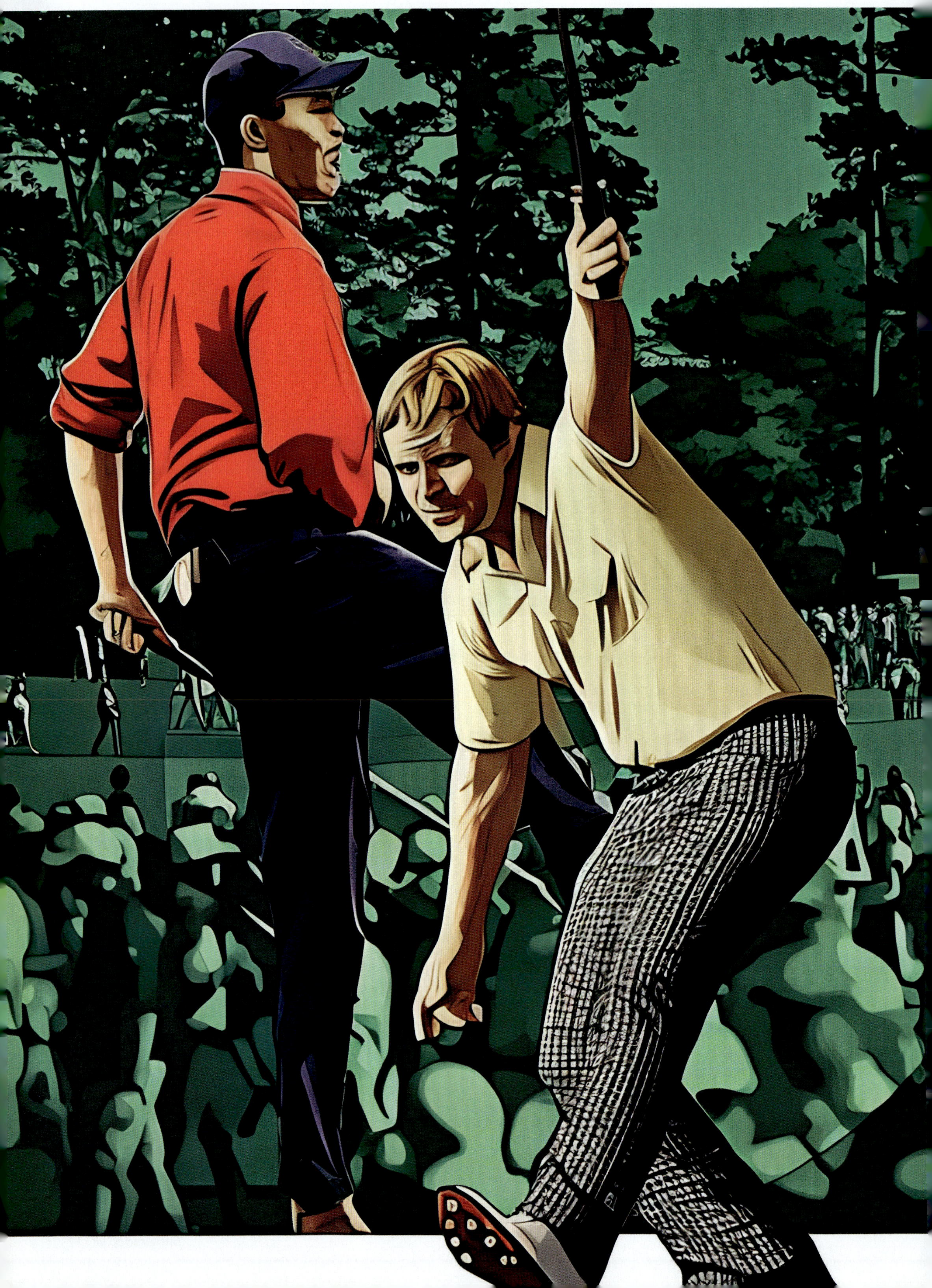

JACK VS TIGER

The Masters that Rocked the World

Not many victories have sent shockwaves through the sport like Jack Nicklaus slipping into a sixth Green Jacket at the age of 46 and a fresh-faced Tiger Woods running riot at Augusta 11 years later. Here, they relive those famous weeks in their own words...

WORDS **ALEX PERRY** PHOTOS **GETTY IMAGES**

1986: Jack's last stand

TIED-60TH. Missed cut. Tied-39th. Missed cut. Tied-47th. Withdrew after round one. Missed cut. That was Jack Nicklaus's form going into the 1986 Masters.

His last top-ten had been the previous September, and you have to go back to the '84 Memorial to find his last PGA Tour victory.

So even the most ardent golf fan would struggle to back him as the world's best rolled into Augusta for the 50th Masters.

The Golden Bear's chances of glory were still slim going into Sunday's round. He trailed 54-hole leader Greg Norman by six, while the likes of Seve Ballesteros, Bernhard Langer, Nick Price, Tom Watson and Sandy Lyle between him and the Australian.

A few hours later, he drove back down Magnolia Lane with a preposterous sixth jacket thanks to one of the finest closing rounds in major championship history.

Using quotes from various interviews over the years, this is Nicklaus's recalling of that famous day...

I really sort of finished my career in 1980, and I wasn't playing so I could be ready for seniors' golf. I just happened to like to play golf and I wanted to be part of it and play a few other things.

I was doing a lot more course design and watching my kids play football, basketball or baseball or golf or whatever it might be. And I was frankly enjoying my life.

Going into the tournament I had no expectations about winning, at all. I wanted to stay part of the Tour. I really loved playing golf.

I was between things in my life. My business was fine but it didn't take up all my time. I'd play some golf, 12 to 14 tournaments a year, not enough to keep me sharp, but enough to be somewhat competitive. I was neither fish nor fowl. I wasn't really a golfer.

I read in the Atlanta paper that 46-year-olds don't win Masters. I agreed.

I got to thinking I was done, through, washed up. I sizzled for a while. But I said to myself, 'I'm not going to quit now, playing the way I'm playing. I've played too well, too long to let a shorter period of bad golf be my last.'

Several things about that Masters were unique. My mother had not been to the Masters since my first one in 1959, and she'd said, 'I want to go to the Masters one more time.'

So she was there, and so was my sister, Marilyn, who had never been to the Masters. Other family members were there, and a bunch of my friends.

I wouldn't wear a shirt at Augusta that you couldn't wear with the Green Jacket. Many years ago the 13-year-old son of Barbara's church minister died of cancer. The boy's name was Craig Smith, and before he passed away he told me he loved watching me play on Sundays, and how he liked it when I wore a yellow shirt because it always seemed to bring me luck.

I remember Barbara telling me to wear yellow that Sunday morning, that it would bring me good luck because of Craig.

Steve [Nicklaus] called me on Sunday morning. He said, 'What do you think, Pops?' I said, 'I think 66 will tie and 65 will win.' He said that's

> **Walking off 18 at Augusta on Sunday is always special. But especially when you're the leader in the clubhouse. This was maybe as fine a round of golf as I've ever played.**

the exact number he had in mind. Go shoot it.

I didn't feel like I could get anything going until the 9th hole. I knocked it in, and I was off. All of a sudden I remembered how to play. I remembered the feeling of being in contention. I remembered the feeling of how you control your emotions and how you enjoy the moment, too.

On 15 there was room on the left and right, and I could go at it. I had a lot of confidence standing over the ball. I chose a 4-iron and hit it solid, very high, and it stopped just a shade past the hole to the left, about 12 feet away. I got a little excited there, a little charged up.

I didn't know how far behind I was, and I didn't care. I just looked around me and I saw all these people excited and having fun. I had done it a lot of times. This is what I'm out here for. This is what I'm supposed to be doing. This is why I'm having so much fun.

When that eagle putt went in, That was the first time I realised I could win the tournament. There weren't many more than Ballesteros in front of me at that point, but I wasn't doing a whole lot of math, I was too busy making birdies.

The 16th is at the bottom of a valley and the noise was deafening. I couldn't hear anything. Nothing! I wasn't trying to think about the leaderboard. All I knew was that I was putting the ball on the green and making birdies.

While the ball was in the air, Jackie said, 'Be right!' I just picked my tee up and said, 'It is.' The remark I made was probably the cockiest I've ever made.

I've had a lot of great receptions at 16 in my life, but that one was pretty special. I made that putt and they were just going bananas.

It was about a 12-foot putt at 17. I don't normally ask Jackie, but I asked and he said, 'Got to go right.' I said, 'I know, but I think it will come back to the left because of Rae's Creek.' There's always that influence back there. So I hit the putt, played it out a couple inches on the left, the ball broke right and the ball sort of turned and sort of straightened out, which meant it was turning back towards Rae's Creek, and I made the putt. I have gone back and putted that putt 100 times since. It's never broken left again.

Walking off 18 at Augusta on Sunday is always special. But especially when you're the leader in the clubhouse. This was maybe as fine a round of golf as I've ever played.

I'm not a big huggy person, but I am with my kids. Jackie and I were both elated at what happened. He's my son. He was with me. That alone was more exciting than the tournament.

I'm sitting in the Jones' Cabin watching. I started getting up and walking around the room, and Norman kept making birdies. And then of course he played the bad second shot at 18.

I didn't expect to win, the press didn't expect me to win, the players didn't expect me to win. But my talents were still there. It was a question of whether I could corral them, keep them in my head, keep myself organised and under control.

Winning it aged 46 does not resonate so much today, simply because of the equipment, but I was playing with a wood driver and a wound golf ball. It was a different game.

People say things like: 'I was in an airport in '86 and cancelled my airplane to watch it.' Or they had to do this, or they had to do that or they had to stop this or had to stop that. It was the most gratifying win of my career.

Obviously all my 18 majors are very special. It is difficult to rank them but the '86 win stands out simply because most of the others I expected to win.

JACK VS TIGER

TALE OF THE TAPE: JACK'S 1986 SCORECARD

ROUND 1

74

ROUND 2

71

ROUND 3

69

ROUND 4

65

TOTAL

279

bunkered.co.uk > 23

1997: Tiger breaks through

IF GENE SARAZEN'S albatross at the 1935 Masters was "the shot heard round the world", then Tiger Woods' 1997 victory at the Masters must have sent shockwaves through the galaxy.

In two attempts as an amateur, Woods had failed to break par at Augusta. But now he was a member of the paid ranks and, although he had only turned pro a few months before, he had already won three PGA Tour titles and moved up to 13th in the world.

Still, stepping into the major winners' circle was going to be a whole knew ball game. Wasn't it?

It certainly looked that way when he needed 40 shots to reach the turn. What happened next defies belief, as he played the remaining 63 holes in 20-under par to finish on -18 and 12 clear of runner up Tom Kite.

It was just the fifth time a major-winning margin had gone into double digits - and the first of the 21st century.

But there was so much more to it than that. Black golfers had only been allowed to compete in the Masters since 1975 - the year Woods was born, incidentally - and racial tensions were so high that the tournament's co-founder, Clifford Roberts, once said: "As long as I'm alive, golfers will be white and caddies will be black."

In his 2017 memoir, Unprecedented: The Masters and Me, Woods wrote: "My biggest hope was we could one day see one another as people and people alone. I wanted us to be colour blind. Twenty years later, that has yet to happen."

This is the story of Woods famous victoy in his own words...

I thought I could win that week. I didn't think I could win by 12 - that was a big ask - but I had been doing things really well.

I shot 59 the week before at Isleworth playing with Mark O'Meara. And I parred both par-fives on the front nine with irons in my hand so it could have been really low. I felt exhilirated.

I played a practice round with Seve and Ollie. It was awesome to hear genius at work, because I had no clue. Seve was incredible. He told me the shots you need to play, the clubs you need to play them with. I'd played practice rounds with Nicklaus, Palmer, Floyd, Couples and Norman, guys who have had a lot of success there. I was lucky enough to pick their brains. I filed everything away.

It was not a good start. I was bewildered and furious. I was hot inside. Just before I stepped on the 10th tee, I let go of that anger and calmed myself. I was thinking of the feeling I had the week before at Isleworth, when I hit one perfect shot after another. The feeling washed over me. My heart rate slowed. I felt free.

Low and behold I hit a great shot down 10 with my 2-iron, and it was a feeling I'd been missing in the first nine holes. And the momentum just completely flipped. I said, 'Just carry this feeling on for the rest of the nine holes.' And I ended up carrying it on for the next 63 holes.

Saturday night, I had to play ping pong, I had to shoot hoops, I had to do everything just not to think about what was going on. I had so much energy.

I didn't wake up early Sunday, which I normally do. I slept throughout the morning and woke up on a perfect schedule.

But the tournament was not over yet. It was a big lead, but I still had to go out and shoot a good number. Whatever I shot, all I wanted is a Green Jacket in my locker.

I was trying to soak it in the best I possibly could, but the tournament wasn't over and in the back of my mind I was thinking, 'I have the chance to do something no one's ever done before. This is a record-breaking deal.' I just didn't want to blow that on the last hole, so making that little four-footer was everything to me.

It was a touching moment for us as a family. It was one of those moments where everyone had just melted away and it was just me and my dad. That was pretty special.

More than anything that week, I was just happy to see dad there, because he'd had open-heart surgery and had complications from that. He went back in the hospital, and he actually died, but they revived him. He wasn't supposed to go to Augusta. He said, 'To hell with you guys, I'm going to support my son!'

Michael Jordan and called to congratulate me, and I was on my way to the press conference when President Clinton called. I talked to him for a bit. That was awfully nice.

I went back to the house and had a few adult beverages. I ended up falling asleep holding the jacket, cuddling it like it was a little bear. I woke up in the morning, still holding it, and said, 'Huh, I did win it.' And boy, my head hurt.

It's hard to believe how much that one tournament has meant so much to me in my life.

> **I thought, 'I have the chance to do something no-one's ever done before. This is a record-breaking deal.' I just didn't want to blow that on the last hole, so making that little four-footer was everything to me.**

JACK VS TIGER

TALE OF THE TAPE: TIGER'S 1997 SCORECARD

ROUND 1

70

ROUND 2

66

ROUND 3

65

ROUND 4

69

TOTAL

270

bunkered.co.uk › 25

HOLD UP... HOW COULD *YOU* WIN ONE?

YES, you could qualify for the Masters. Simply enter The Amateur, run by the R&A. You'll need a handicap of either +1.5 or be inside the WAGR top 2000 at date of entry. Win that and you'll get entry to the following year's Masters (if you stay amateur). You then get unlimited practice rounds at Augusta National in the lead-up (of which you will likely take advantage) and then you just need to beat the best players in the world. If you believe in yourself, anything is possible. Miley Cyrus said that. It's true.

THE HISTORY OF THE **GREEN JACKET**

The history of the Green Jacket

It's the most famous item of clothing in sport, but how did the humble Green Jacket become one of golf's most prized possessions?

WORDS **ALEX PERRY**   PHOTOS **GETTY IMAGES**

THE STORY of the Green Jacket begins, would you believe, in England. When legendary amateur Bobby Jones arrived at Royal Liverpool Golf Club to take part in the 1930 Open Championship, something caught his eye during a pre-tournament drinks reception.

Club captain, Kenneth Stoker, and his predecessors were wearing matching red jackets.

Jones liked what he saw, and the story goes that Mr Stoker promised the American that, should he win that week's Open, he would gift him his prized garment. A few days later, Jones was on his way back across the Atlantic with not only his third Claret Jug but a blazer of his own courtesy of his new friend in Hoylake.

Three years later, Jones would open his own golf club – Augusta National – and pitched the idea of matching jackets for members. Red, yellow, and, of course, 'Georgia Peach' were put on the table, before the voting committee settled on green to match the lush surroundings.

When The Masters – known as the Augusta National Invitation Tournament for its first six iterations – was inaugurated a few months later, club members wore the woolen jackets to distinguish themselves from patrons.

In 1949, it was decided that each Masters champion would take home a Green Jacket of his own, with all past winners retroactively receiving one.

BADGE OF HONOUR

Let's get technical for a moment.

The Augusta National Green Jacket is a three-button, single-breasted, single-vented blazer with a notch lapel.

The tropical wool fabric used is produced by Victor Frostman Inc. in Dublin, Georgia, around 90 miles south of Augusta, while the jackets themselves are made by Hamilton Tailoring Company in Cincinnati, Ohio.

An embroidered patch featuring the club's famous logo adorns the left breast pocket, as do the brass buttons, which are custom-made by the Waterbury Company of Connecticut.

Each Green Jacket, which has its owner's name stitched on the inside lining, takes approximately one month and costs around $250 to make.

OBEY THE RULES

Only one Green Jacket is allowed to leave the property at Augusta National – and that is the one owned by the reigning Masters champion.

For one year, the winner of men's golf's opening major is permitted to take the jacket home and do as they wish. That's why you often see players on talk shows or at sporting events while in their newly-acquired clothing.

But from the moment they return for the following year's Masters, it is kept safely in the Champions Locker Room for each time they visit the famed Georgia club.

Of course, not everyone follows the rules. Legend has it that it was Nick Faldo who normalised wearing the Green Jacket for various press appearances, which the board at ANGC reportedly didn't like, while Seve Ballesteros is said to have flat out refused when asked to return his jacket after his Masters wins in 1980 and '82.

But it was Gary Player who most famously found himself on the wrong side of the then Augusta chairman Clifford Roberts. When the first non-American Masters champion received a phone call in his native South Africa asking why his jacket was on the other side of the Atlantic, Player replied: "Fine, Mr Roberts. If you want it, come and fetch it!"

The 1961 champion agreed not to wear his Green Jacket in public again and, from the following year, stricter rules were put in place.

SALE OF THE CENTURY

There was more controversy in 1994 when a genuine Augusta National Green Jacket turned up in a charity shop in Canada. Bought by a local journalist, who couldn't believe his luck at the $5 asking price, it was re-sold in 2017 by Florida-based Green Jacket Auctions for a whopping $139,000.

This tipped off Augusta National, which had trademarked the name 'Green Jacket' seven years prior and set its legal team into action. The company is now known as Golden Age Auctions, while Mullion Golf Club in Cornwall also received a cease and desist to stop offering green jackets to winners of its own annual tournament.

"They're an 800-pound gorilla," one legal opponent once told *Golf* magazine. "They try to bully you."

However, that didn't stop the hammer coming down on a Green Jacket owned by Horton Smith for his victory in the inaugural Masters for a cool $682,229 in 2013, while Jones' blazer had fetched $310,700 two years before.

JACK TO SQUARE ONE

No-one has won the Masters more than Jack Nicklaus – and yet he never got his hands on his own Green Jacket until relatively recently.

When the Golden Bear, who triumphed six times at Augusta, won his first, the powers-that-be didn't have the right size, so they ended up lending him one which was far too big.

"They must have thought I was huge," Nicklaus joked years later. "It hung off me like an old blanket."

For his second and third wins, Nicklaus borrowed the jacket off Thomas Dewey, a New York governor, to wear in public while the original 46-long hung in his locker.

"Nobody ever spoke to me about it – and I was never going to say anything," Nicklaus recalled.

Then, ahead of his fourth win in '72, and with the now late Mr Dewey buried in his beloved blazer, Nicklaus decided to have his own made by one of his sponsors

> **"A genuine Augusta National Green Jacket turned up in a charity shop in Canada. It was bought by a local journalist for $5 and sold at auction for $139,000.**

THE HISTORY OF THE GREEN JACKET

EURO-FLASH
Left: Europe's first five Masters champions (L-R) Nick Faldo, Sandy Lyle, Ian Woosnam, Bernhard Langer, and Seve Ballesteros; Below: Tiger Woods in his Green Jacket

– clothing company Hart, Shaffner & Marx. Even though it was the wrong shade of green – Pantone 342, if you're wondering – the replica remained until 1997, when Nicklaus finally mentioned it to then Augusta chairman Jackson Stevens, who immediately requested one to be made.

But Nicklaus declined the belated offer. "It was such a great story," he said. "I didn't want to ruin it." Perhaps that's why now there is a field on the registration form invitees which fill out ahead of the Masters that asks for their jacket size.

THE OTHER MASTERS PRIZES

TROPHY
Made of more than 900 pieces of silver and featuring the names of every Masters champion and runner-up, this replica of the Augusta clubhouse remains on the grounds, with a small sterling silver version handed out to the winner.

GOLD MEDAL
The Masters champion also receives a 3.4-inch gold medal, which weighs around 65 grams. It includes a rendering of Founders Circle, which is the area located between Magnolia Lane and the clubhouse.

SILVER MEDAL
The runner-up also gets a medal, only silver – for hopefully obvious reasons. He also receives a lovely salver.

LOW AMATEUR TROPHY
Also known as the Silver Cup, this has been handed out to the best-performing amateur of the week – provided they make the cut – since 1952.

PAR-3 CONTEST TROPHY
The winner of the Wednesday afternoon hit-and-giggle has famously never gone on to win the Green Jacket in the same year, but they are presented with a crystal bowl embossed with the Masters logo.

CRYSTAL VASE
This is for the golfer who posts the lowest round on each tournament day.

CRYSTAL BOWL
This is for anyone who makes a hole-in-one or an albatross during the Masters.

CRYSTAL GOBLETS
And finally, a goblet for anyone making an eagle in tournament play.

HORTON SMITH

The original *Master*

The remarkable story of the first-ever Masters champion and golf's original 'Boy Wonder', Horton Smith

WORDS **MICHAEL McEWAN** PHOTOS **GETTY IMAGES**

THE ORIGINAL MASTER

BOY WONDER
Horton Smith, pictured at Augusta in 1960, won the first and third editions of the Masters.

IT WASN'T SUPPOSED to happen this way. Bobby Jones, the founder and co-designer of the course, was meant to win the inaugural Augusta National Invitation Tournament.

It was to be his swansong, his fond and final farewell to the game some four years after he had formally retired after completing the 'Impregnable Quadrilateral of Golf' at the age of 28. Golf, though, seldom accommodates schmaltz. Ye Gods are significantly less predisposed to sentimentality.

And so, almost three-quarters of a century after Old Tom Morris had been edged out for glory in the first edition of the Open Championship, an event he had helped create, Jones was left to watch another man win the first edition of the event that would, in short order, become one of golf's most prestigious tournaments.

That man was a 26-year-old called Horton Smith.

Born on May 22, 1908, in Springfield, Missouri, Horton was the second of two boys born to Perry and Ann Smith. The couple owned a farm, around seven miles from town, on which Horton and his brother Ren would work.

When the boys were still young, Perry and Ann bought a new farm closer to the town and just half a mile from Springfield Country Club. It was here that Horton was introduced to golf.

At the age of 11, he started caddying for club members, earning 25 cents for nine holes. He also began to play a bit and, every day after school, he would strap his clubs to his back, hop on his bike, and head to the course.

Before long, the Smith family joined Springfield Country Club, which gave Horton unfettered access to the course and its facilities. Head professional Neil Crose was quick to spot the young man's talent and took him under his wing. In 1921, at the age of 13, he finished runner-up to older brother Ren in the club's junior championship, going one better the following year.

Two years later, the siblings were given the opportunity to caddie for Walter Hagen – already a four-time major champion – and Australia-born golfer-cum-actor Joe Kirkwood when the pair played an exhibition match in Joplin. At the end of the match, Hagen handed Smith some balls and wooden tees and the pair subsequently struck up a friendship

bunkered.co.uk > 31

that would last for many years.

The same year, at the age of 15, Smith won the Springfield Country Club Championship and Springfield City Championship. He also broke the course record at his home club, carding a remarkable 58, which included playing the par-31 front nine in just 26 shots.

After finishing high school, he attended the State Teachers' College in his hometown. However, his passion for golf continued to burn brightly and so, against his father's wishes, he abandoned his education to take up a post as assistant to his mentor Crose at Springfield Country Club.

In 1927, he accepted his first head professional job, moving up-state to Sedalia Country Club. The same year, he qualified for his first US Open, finishing 44th at Oakmont as Tommy Armour won the first of his three major titles.

The following year, having spent much of the winter playing in events across the country, Smith moved to Joplin to become the head pro at Oak Hill Country Club. Within months, he had won his first professional title, claiming the $1,000 Oklahoma City Open. He repeated the trick just weeks later, taking the Catalina Open at Hagen's expense.

Holding a three-shot lead, Smith went back out onto the course to watch Hagen play his last three holes.

"What did you shoot?" Hagen asked him.

When Smith told him, Hagen is said to have replied: "Well, I guess I need to shoot a three, a two and a one to beat you."

He birdied the par-4 16th and the par-3 17th. That left just the par-3 18th. Before hitting his tee shot, Hagen sent his caddie down to the green to tend the flag. He took dead aim but the ball flew past the flag, handing victory to his former teenage caddie.

It was in 1929 that Smith enjoyed his big breakthrough. The tall, smooth-swinging 21-year-old played 22 events on the fledgling PGA Tour, winning eight times and banking more than $15,000 – almost $400,000 in today's money – to finish top of the money list. He got there in no small part thanks to what some described as his "almost supernatural" putting ability. Unsurprisingly, he was voted onto the US Ryder Cup team that year and, to date, he remains the youngest man ever to represent America in the biennial contest.

In the 1930 Savannah Open, he became the last man ever to beat Bobby Jones in formal competition.

Four years later, in March 1934, he was one of 60 professionals and 12 amateurs invited by Jones to play in the inaugural Augusta National Invitation Tournament. The field was a who's who of the game, featuring the likes of Hagen, Gene Sarazen, and Harry Cooper. However, it was the course that was arguably the biggest star.

Built on the site of the old Fruitland Nursery, Augusta National had opened just 15 months earlier and had already created plenty of buzz. With this all going on, it was little wonder the tournament was chosen to be the focus of the first national radio broadcast of a golf event.

At the time, the course's two nines were back to front. Players started on the tenth, 'Camellia', and finished on the ninth, 'Carolina Cherry'. It switched to its current configuration in time for the 1935 tournament.

With much of the focus on Jones, who laboured to a first round 75, Smith finished the first round tied for the lead with Jimmy Hines and Emmet French. The trio were just a shot ahead of a cluster of players, including Walter Hagen.

With the tournament played over four consecutive days – unusual for golf tournaments at the time, which typically consisted

LIKELY LADS
Right: Fomer champions Byron Nelson, Jimmy Demaret, Henry Picard, Horton Smith, Ben Hogan, Craig Wood, Claude Harmon, Gene Sarazen and Sam Snead pictured in 1954. Below: Smith tucks in to a famous Augusta breakfast.

THE ORIGINAL MASTER

of back-to-back days of 36 holes – Smith carded a level-par 72 in difficult conditions the following day to hold a one-shot lead at halfway.

He maintained his lead after 54 holes, shooting a two-under 70 to lead Billy Burke by one going into the final round.

With the chasing pack refusing to give up their pursuit, Smith ultimately sealed the victory with a 20-foot birdie putt on the penultimate hole, finishing one ahead of Craig Wood.

He and Augusta National were an almost instant love-match. "To me, the course has character, individuality and personality," he said. "It is one of the few courses that really presents two games on almost every hole; a game to reach the greens and another to figure the ever-challenging contours after reaching the greens."

However, there was no Green Jacket for him that year. It wasn't until 1949 that the most famous piece of sports clothing was first presented, whereupon all previous champions were retroactively awarded one of their own.

By that time, Smith was a two-time champion, having won the tournament again in 1936. It was during that event that he met Barbara Bourne, the heiress to the Singer Sewing Machine estate. The couple married in 1938 and had a son, Alfred, in 1943. However, they divorced two years later, Barbara petitioning for an end to marriage on the grounds of "mental cruelty".

As his playing career wound down, Smith took on more of an involvement in the governance of the game and, in 1952, became president of the Professional Golfers' Association. His three terms at the helm of the organisation coincided with some significant changes, not least the inclusion of African-Americans on the tour. When former world heavyweight champion Joe Louis was banned from playing in the San Diego Open, Smith told the tournament committee to incorporate an "approved entry clause", which would allow individual tournaments to invite whoever they wanted to take part. That change allowed Louis to play.

Following the 1957 Masters, Smith developed a persistent cough, which was later diagnosed as Hodgkin's disease and required an operation to remove part of his lung. He recovered to play at Augusta in 1958, continuing his streak of playing in every edition of the Masters. He extended that run of consecutive appearances to 27 before he died on October 15, 1963, aged just 55.

He was the first of the former Masters champions to pass away, followed by Craig Wood in 1968 and Jimmy Demaret in 1983.

All told, he won 36 events and, in addition to his two Masters wins, racked up 17 other major championship top-ten finishes.

In September 2013, Smith's Green Jacket, awarded in 1949 for his Masters wins in 1934 and 1936, and which had been in the possession of his brother's stepchildren, sold at auction for over $682,000 – the highest price ever paid for a piece of golf memorabilia.

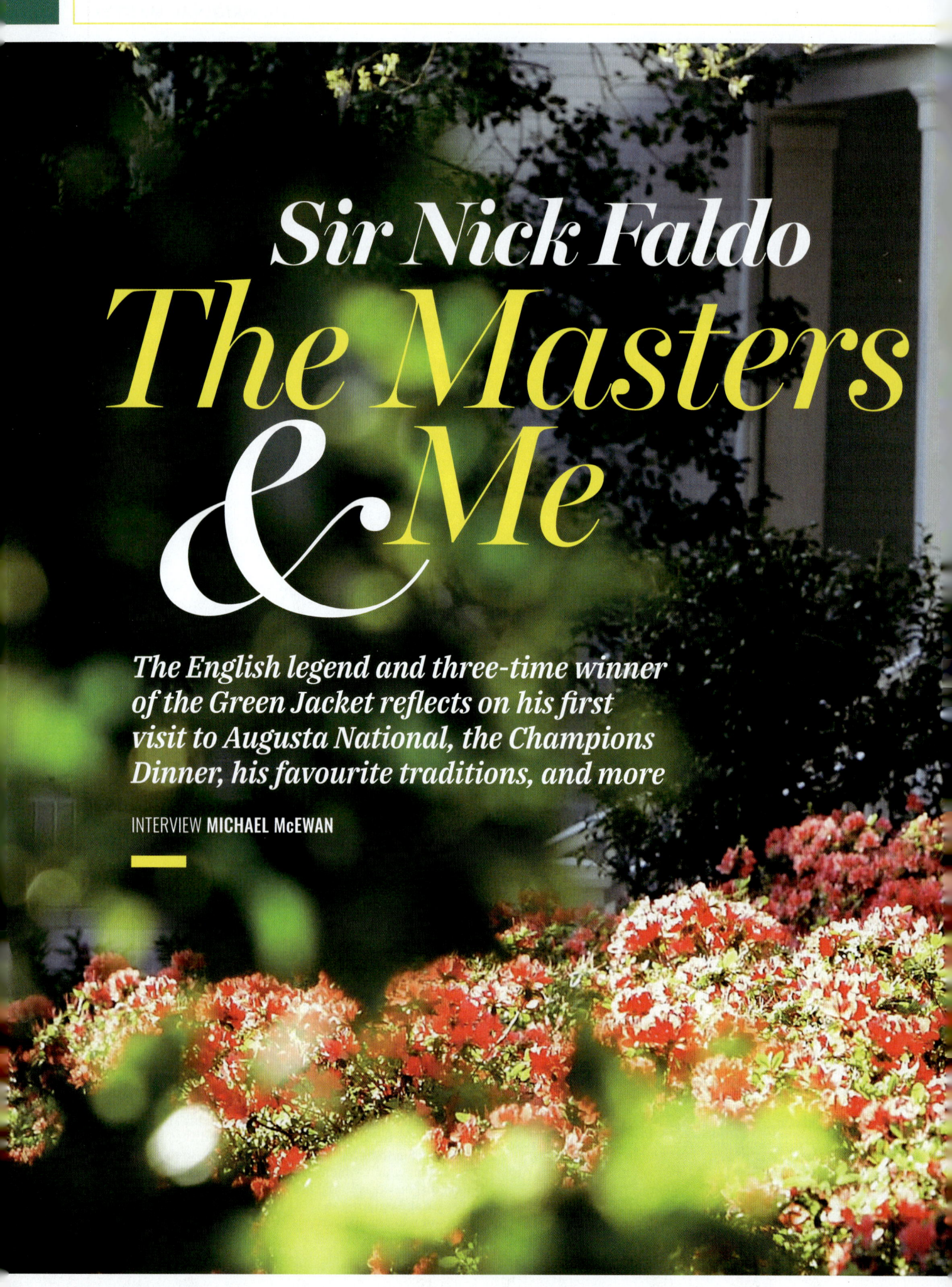

Sir Nick Faldo
The Masters & Me

The English legend and three-time winner of the Green Jacket reflects on his first visit to Augusta National, the Champions Dinner, his favourite traditions, and more

INTERVIEW **MICHAEL McEWAN**

SIR NICK FALDO THE MASTERS & ME

IT WAS THE GREAT GENE SARAZEN who once remarked: "You don't come to Augusta to find your game. You come here because you've got one."

The list of former Masters champions bears out the veracity of the great man's sentiment.

Taking his rightful place among them is Sir Nick Faldo. Consider for a moment the identities of the three players who have won the first men's major of the season more often: Jack Nicklaus, Tiger Woods, Arnold Palmer – arguably the three greatest and most influential players in the history of the game.

Only seventeen players in the history of the game have won the Masters more than once. Of those, only eight have won it at least three times. Make no mistake, whenever the history of this tournament is written, Sir Nick's name will figure prominently.

Who better, then, to ask for an insight into the most anticipated week of the year?

For those of us who'll never experience it, how special is it to be able to call yourself a Masters champion?
It's a huge honour. The quality of the way they do things there is just on another level.

I remember going to Berckmans Place when it opened a few years ago. That's one of their corporate hospitality areas. It's tucked away among the trees beside the fifth fairway and, honestly, it's as though they've built another clubhouse.

They've got restaurants in there, putting greens, a museum and everything is done to a standard that you cannot believe. It's seven-star stuff. It really is.

It's a corporate ticket, so obviously it's expensive, but you don't pay for anything once you're in and the service is magnificent and everybody's attitude is amazing.

I actually got choked up because I thought about how proud I am to be part of an organisation that does things the way they do. People always say if you're going to do something, do it right.

Well, they exemplify that like you can't believe.

I mean this in the nicest possible way, but Augusta can be quite an intimidating place at first, can't it?
Yeah, you know it took me years to get comfortable enough to wear my Green Jacket outside of the clubhouse. It actually came from my son, Matthew. We were there, sitting on the back lawn and he had one of his mates with him and he said, 'Where's the jacket?' I said, 'It's in my locker.' He said, 'Will you put it on?' I said, 'Sure, alright.' So, I went and got it, put it on and we sat and had lunch.

That's probably about ten years ago now but that was the first time I'd got comfortable really being part of it. It's such a special thing.

The fact you get to wear it because you're a champion, you can wear it until the day you roll over.

What do you remember of the first time you played the course? Did it live up to expectations?
It was really daunting. The green speeds, the slopes, you've got no idea where to hit it, where to bail out, that sort of thing. So, in that first year, you make all of those straight and obvious mistakes and come back the next year and try not to repeat them.

bunkered.co.uk > 35

It's hard for anybody who hasn't played there to appreciate just how blisteringly quick some of the greens can get. You get a six- or eight-footer straight downhill but, because of the character of the greens, they just keep running at that percentage.

It's never a case of, 'With a bit of luck, it'll just stop four feet past the hole.' No, it won't. That's the scary part. If it's going past, it's going past. There's an art to it. Four feet past at Augusta is very good. Seriously. If you're really trying to get a perfect weight, there are going to be a lot of putts that you won't be able to put a stroke on.

What's the biggest surprise you get when you first walk onto the course?
The undulations, definitely. People don't appreciate how it goes charging down the hill. You stand outside the clubhouse and it just goes straight down across the ninth. It's a good couple of hundred-foot of a drop. So, if you miss a green, you can be a good eight or nine feet below it depending on the undulations. You can't really grasp that watching on TV.

Do you have a favourite spot on the property?
I'd have to say the 11th hole, for pretty obvious reasons! [Faldo won his first Green Jacket in 1989 with a birdie on the 11th, the second hole of a playoff with Scott Hoch. He had bogeyed the hole in all four regulation rounds.]

I did a piece for CBS on the 30th anniversary of that win. I walked down the hole wearing my jacket and that choked me up as well.

I'm an emotional petal under certain circumstances! But that place will get you. It's so special.

Augusta is well known for traditions. Do you have a favourite?
I do actually. I'm very lucky, in the run-up to the Masters, past winners are allowed to take a guest to play the course with them.

People think that because I've won there, I'm a member. I'm actually not. If I want to go and play Augusta National tomorrow, I still have to play with a member.

But on that occasion, I'm allowed to bring a guest. So, I take my boy, Matthew, and we've been doing that now for several years, ever since he turned 18.

We arrive the night before, get up early, have breakfast at the club, play 18 holes on the big course, have a spot of lunch and then go play the par-3 course. It's lovely. The best bit is arguably arriving first thing in the morning, picking your spot on the corner of the upstairs balcony in the clubhouse and looking out across the property, across all the umbrellas, the patrons slowly making their way in. Trust me, that doesn't get old.

Yeah, it's very, very cool.

The Champions' Dinner is another tradition that people seem to get a kick out of. What's it like inside that room?
Well, Sam Snead used to tell the most risqué stories and then Lord Byron [Nelson] would announce, 'That's the end of the meeting!'

Things went a bit quiet for a while but, you know what, it was probably after Arnold [Palmer] passed that it turned around again. That first year was particularly emotional. People were telling stories about Arnold and who he was, what he was like, the things he did. More than anything, we rib each other, which is a lot of fun.

Jack [Nicklaus] will sit there and start talking about equalling the course record in 1965 on his way to winning his first Green Jacket, and he'll go, 'Well, you know, I thought the course was playing pretty easy!' And everyone will boo him and throws their napkins

NICK'S PICS
Clockwise from main: At Augusta National in 2024 with wife Lindsay; preparing to serve fish and chips at the Champions Dinner in 1997; signing autographs for fans after winning the 1989 Masters.

SIR NICK FALDO THE MASTERS & ME

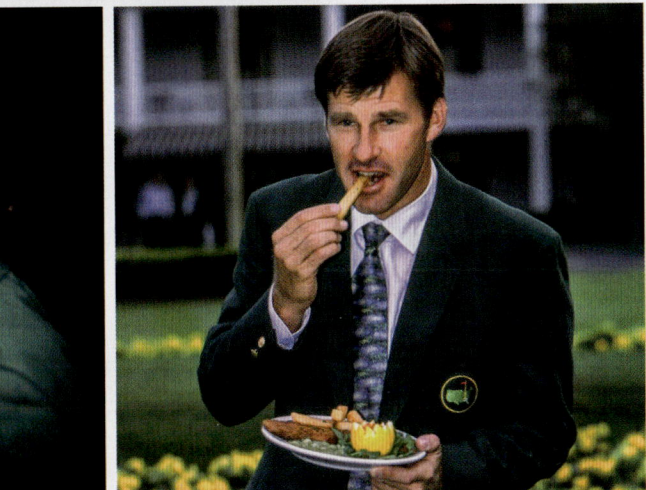

at him, stuff like that. I sit next to Gary [Player] and he's always telling Hogan stories, which is always fun. It's always a great evening.

You've been to 30 different dinners now. Which menus stand out as being particularly good?
[Ben] Crenshaw did a really good Texas BBQ. Vijay [Singh] has some friends who are Thai restaurateurs so he kind of started the tradition that we have crudités on the balcony before we go in for dinner, so we have lovely crab, sushi, ham and so on, which is always great. For my third dinner, I flew over Harry Ramsden cod fillets, real chips, mushy peas and loads of Sarson's vinegar. In my opinion, that's the third best dinner we ever had because everybody had it and everybody loved it. It was really cool, especially when the waiter came round with the mushy peas and said [puts on thick American drawl], 'Can I interest any of y'all in this green stuff?' I said, 'That's mushy peas!' He said, 'Mushy what?'

You would have to think that, as a three-time champion, your name will enter the discussion to become an honorary starter. Is that something you'd welcome?
Gee, are you kidding? I'd be honoured to accept that.
I'm not sure if they're waiting until I'm 70 or something but I hope they don't wait too long because I want to be able to pound one out there, you know?
But in all seriousness, as you can imagine, that would be an incredible honour. I've always said that as long as my legs still work, I'll be at Augusta every year.

Pimento cheese sandwiches: thumbs up or thumbs down?
Yeah, they're alright. They're quite tangy but that's fine, I like tangy cheese. I don't like the white bread, though. Why have they got it on white bread? Now that I'm on a keto diet, I can't have bread so I'd probably scrape the pimento out and have it on an avocado or something.

What would you tell a player taking part in the Masters for the first time?
Go there early. Just get there and get the aura over and done with. The first time I went, I couldn't handle it. I seem to remember getting in on the Monday after racing up from playing the Greater Greensboro Open and, honestly, it was just too much. So, I would go in early, get your bearings, study a few downhill putts and let yourself be a little overwhelmed by the whole place and all so that, when it's time to get to work, that's out of your system.

Finally, what one word would you choose to describe the Masters?
Well, I'd have to go with a good British word, so how about 'fabulous'? Because it really is.

> **Becoming an honorary starter would be incredible. I've always said that as long as my legs still work, I'll be at Augusta every year.**

bunkered.co.uk > 37

THE HOMETOWN BOY

LARRY MIZE

In 1987, Larry Mize lived his boyhood dream when he became the first golfer from Augusta to win the Masters. In this interview, he reflects on the "greatest blessing" of his career.

WORDS **MICHAEL McEWAN** — PHOTOS **GETTY IMAGES**

THE CHAMPION LARRY MIZE

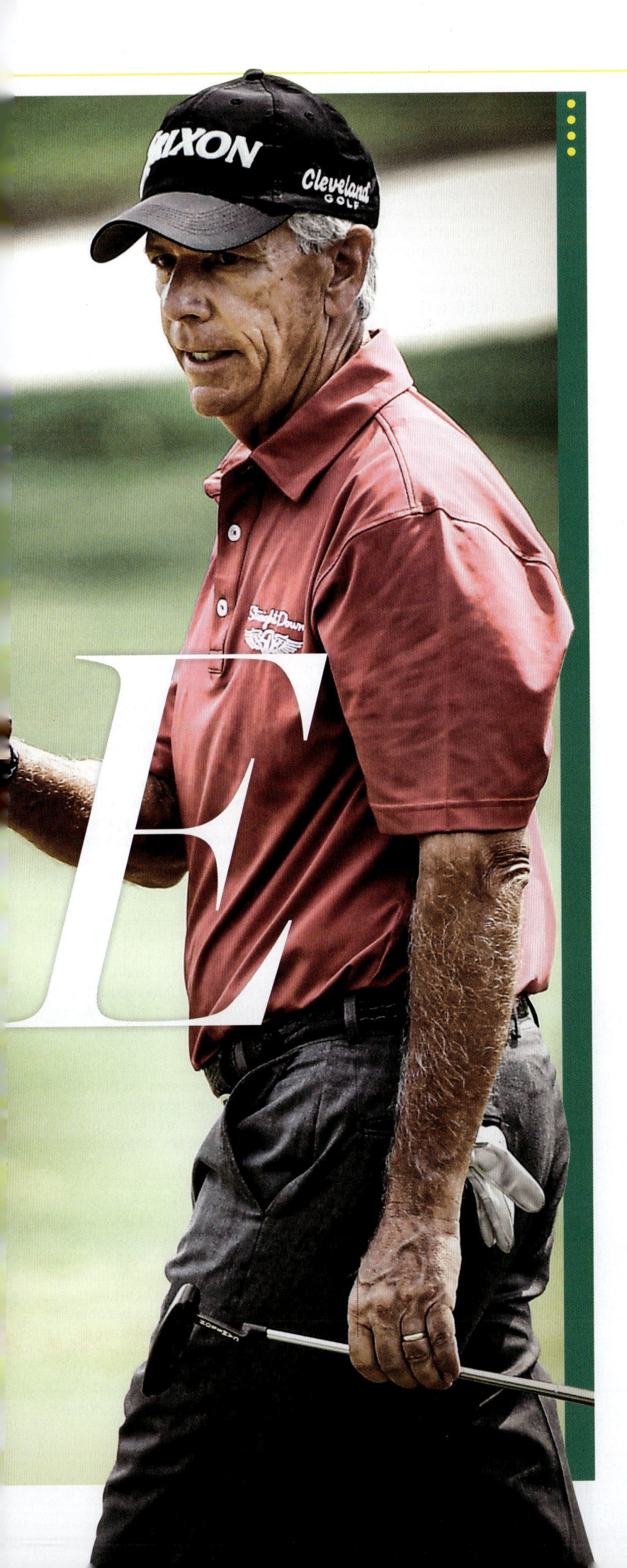

THE INSTANT HE HIT IT, HE KNEW. The fact that the ball landed on the exact spot he had picked out in his mind's eye only strengthened his conviction. This could be it. This could be the moment this hometown boy won the Masters.

Truth be told, there was no other shot on. A poor second into the 11th – the second hole of a sudden-death playoff – left him with absolutely no alternative. His opponent, Greg Norman, was just on the green, around 40 feet from the hole, and putting for birdie. He had to assume the Australian would, at worst, make four, so he would need to do likewise. That meant playing the perfect third from purgatory, knowing that either heaven or hell awaited.

He couldn't land the ball on the green because, with the speed and slope of the slick surfaces, there's no way it would finish on the short stuff. It was for the same reason he couldn't pull his 8-iron and play a little bump and run.

No, the only option was to grab his 56° wedge – the only wedge in his bag – and try to check the ball once, if not twice, into the bank in front of the green. Beyond that, it was up to gravity and fate to do the rest.

He executed it just the way he wanted and, as the ball tracked towards the hole, on a seemingly inexorable collision course with it, he froze.

It was happening. *It was really happening*.

The ball disappeared below the ground and the roars went up. So, too, did his wedge, tossed high into the air as euphoria consumed him.

When Norman failed to convert his putt, the 1987 Masters Tournament was over.

Larry Mize, born in Augusta 28 years earlier, was the champion.

GROWING UP IN AUGUSTA, the Masters was a big deal for Mize and his classmates. For one thing, it signalled spring break. For another, it was a week when the world's best golfers came to town, bringing with them the eyes of the world. "It was something we looked forward to every year," he recalls.

In the early '70s, tickets were much easier to come by than they are now. He and his father Charles were members at Augusta Country Club, the course that backs onto 'Amen Corner', and so the Masters was, as Mize puts it, a great opportunity to "sit in the bleachers and try to learn some stuff".

He saw all the greats up close. Players like Gene Littler and Sam Snead, Arnold Palmer and Henry Picard. The one he was most excited to watch, though, was Jack Nicklaus. "He was so powerful. He could hit the ball so far and was such a fantastic champion."

When he turned 13, Mize applied to be a scoreboard operator at the tournament. He lucked-out, getting assigned to the third hole. "It was great fun. You got a free ticket and a free lunch. There were two different shifts – early and late – and no matter which one you got, you were always able to watch the leaders play most of their rounds afterwards."

All of which makes his win in 1987 even more remarkable. He had made his debut in the tournament only three years earlier, courtesy of his 1983 Memphis Classic victory, and had finished in a more-than-respectable tie for 11th.

But winning? Winning was another matter altogether. Entering the week of the 1987 tournament, Mize was 36th on the OWGR. By the end of the regulation 72 holes, he was tied for the lead with two of the top-three players on the rankings, No.1 Norman and No.3 Seve Ballesteros. As good as a player as he was and as well as he had played, he wasn't expected to win the subsequent playoff.

"I wasn't really thinking about any of that," he admits. "I had been in a six-man playoff with Greg at the Kemper Open the previous year, which he had won, so I had experience of being in that situation with him before. And Seve, he and I had played a lot of golf together by that point, too, so I naturally respected him and knew exactly what he was capable of. But hey, we had played 72 holes and there was nothing to separate us. So, I wasn't thinking about their reputations or rankings or whatever. My focus was solely on the playoff and making sure I took care of my own business."

A bogey on the first extra hole, the tenth, saw Ballesteros eliminated. It was now a straight shootout between Mize and Norman. Both found the fairway off the tee at 11 but when Mize missed the green to the left with his second and Norman just about clung on to the putting surface with own approach, it was very much 'Advantage Australia'.

"I was pretty disappointed with myself after my second, but I had to forget about it quickly and, when I got down there, it was clear there was really only one shot I could play. In a way, that was to my advantage. I mean, yes, it was an extraordinarily difficult shot but the worst thing you can be around any golf course – and particularly Augusta National – is indecisive. It was do or die. I knew I had to hit an aggressive shot but one judged to perfection to put the pressure back on Greg."

Perfection it was. In the TV booth, the CBS commentators fell silent for 41 seconds after the ball hit the hole, rendered speechless by the improbability of what they had just witnessed. When they finally did speak, Steve Melnyk – himself a native of Georgia – did so for everybody. "Words," he gasped, "do not do justice to the greatness of that shot."

Even now, almost 40 years later, Mize admits he struggles to articulate the moment the ball hit the hole. "It was total excitement, total elation. I mean, it's..." He pauses. "It's almost indescribable. It was a dream come true just to play in the Masters, so to win it was beyond my wildest expectations."

One suspects he's been lost in this moment many times in the last three-and-a-half decades.

"You know, the Masters is a special tournament for any golfer to win but for a kid from Augusta, it's unbelievable. Undoubtedly, it's the highlight of my career. Nothing I could do, indeed nothing I ever did, would top it. It has been the greatest blessing of my professional life."

The almost-absurd perfection of the day was completed by Nicklaus, whom Mize had so enjoyed watching on the grounds as a kid, helping him into the Green Jacket. The winner of the tournament in record-breaking fashion a year earlier, Nicklaus was on hand to congratulate him at the prize-giving ceremony.

"I can't remember exactly what he said but it was along the lines of 'you played like a champion today'," Mize recalls. "He couldn't have been nicer and to get that kind of compliment from somebody I had looked up to for so long just made the whole thing so much more special."

As a champion, Mize enjoys a lifetime exemption to the Masters, which he recently gave up, as well as many other perks. One of those is an invitation to the Champions' Dinner, held on the Tuesday of Masters week. It is, in effect, a club within a club and, each year, the previous year's champion sets the menu. Over the years, Mize has seen an array of eclectic dishes put in front of the former winners.

"I remember after one of his wins, [Nick] Faldo served a Shepherd's Pie, which was fantastic," Mize explains. "I mean, I love meat and potatoes, so it was always going to get my approval, right? Vijay [Singh] did a fantastic Thai dish. Another year, Phil [Mickelson] served a wonderful pasta meal. It's always a fantastic night. The only thing I couldn't bring myself to try was Sandy Lyle's haggis. I wanted to but I just couldn't pull the trigger."

Mize played in his 40th and final Masters in 2023. He didn't missed a single edition since he made his debut in 1984. For context, Phil Mickelson made 27 consecutive appearances between 1995 and 2021. Tiger Woods' best streak ended at 19 when he sat out 2014. Jack Nicklaus could 'only' manage 40. The record for consecutive starts is held by the late Arnold Palmer, who made 50.

Mize has seen many of the game's greatest players make legends of themselves at Augusta and hopes to be around to see many more follow suit.

One of those heavily fancied to do so is Bryson DeChambeau, a man whose prodigious power has made him a favourite for a Green Jacket. How the tournament committee might mitigate his prospects has become a hot topic of discussion, with many speculating that significant alterations to the course might be required to keep it relevant. Mize doesn't

OTHER SHOCK WINNERS

Making just his second Masters appearance, Danny Willett capitalised on a back nine collapse by defending champ Jordan Spieth to win in 2016.

He's well-known now but Zach Johnson was a 125-1 rank outsider with only one PGA Tour title to his name when he won in 2007.

In 1979, just his fifth season on tour, Fuzzy Zoeller became the first golfer to win on their Masters debut since Gene Sarazen 44 years earlier.

40 ‹ bunkered.co.uk

THE CHAMPION LARRY MIZE

believe major changes are needed.

"There's so much more to Augusta National than being able to drive it big," he says. "It's a true 'second shot' golf course.

"Hit it as far as you want but if your shot into the green isn't very good, you're not going to do well.

"The list of champions over the years demonstrates that. Seve, Jack, Arnold, Bernhard [Langer], Tiger – all good drivers of the ball but exceptional iron players.

"You know, people talk about Bryson and they like to mention what club he's hitting into greens. To me, it's not the club but where you're hitting it from that matters. Positions are so important and what doesn't get talked about enough is the fact that Bryson, with his length, could find some pretty awkward positions if he doesn't drive it perfect. So, perhaps they'll need to make some little tweaks here and there but I don't think they need to do anything hugely significant."

You can hear the smile in Mize's voice as he talks about his favourite spots at Augusta – on the property, it's the par-3 course; on the course itself, its down by the 13th tee – and his favourite things to eat and drink within the grounds. "Give me a grape juice and ginger ale, and a ham and cheese on rye and I'm happy," he laughs. It's a tournament that has had a significant impact on his life and career and, for that, he's hugely grateful. In his home, his Masters trophy is on display in the break room and the wall of his study contains a framed picture of Nicklaus congratulating him on his win.

Come April, he'll return to his hometown, turn off Washington and drive up Magnolia Lane. Inside the clubhouse at the top of the most famous 330 yards in golf, he'll go up to the second floor where he'll push through the doors and into the Champions Locker Room. A brass plaque bearing his name will direct Mize to his own locker, within which he'll find his Green Jacket waiting for him.

"How does it feel to put it on? Very nice." Once again, the smile in his voice is unmistakable. "It's so special. To go there on the Tuesday morning and to put it on, it's – it's hard to explain what it means to me.

"Yeah, I'm a lucky man."

THAT WINNING FEELING
Left: Larry Mize celebrates after chipping in to beat Greg Norman in 1987.
Below: Mize rejoices in his Masters win in 1987 with caddie Scotty Steele. He made his final appearance in the 2023 Masters.

NEARLY MEN

THE BEST PLAYERS
never to win
THE MASTERS

Winning a Green Jacket isn't for everyone. Just ask this nonet of the game's finest.

WORDS **MICHAEL McEWAN** & **ALEX PERRY** PHOTOS **GETTY IMAGES**

MOST GOLF FANS would agree that to be considered as one of the greatest of all time, you have to have pulled on the famous Green Jacket as a winner of the Masters.

Despite this, some of the best and most talented golfers in the history of the game – multiple major winners amongst them – have failed to win one of golf's most coveted prizes.

Lee Trevino

ONE OF ONLY four players to have won the US Open, The Open and the PGA Championship twice each – but Trevino had a complicated relationship with Augusta National, posting only two top-tens in 20 starts. After the 1969 Masters, he famously said: "Don't talk to me about the Masters. I'm never going to play there again. They can invite me all they want, but I'm not going back. It's just not my type of course." As a fader of the ball, he felt his game didn't suit the course. He subsequently skipped several editions of the event, which he has since described as "the greatest mistake I've made in my career".

BEST PLAYERS **NEVER TO WIN**

Greg Norman

WHAT IS THERE to be said about Norman's love-hate relationship with the Masters that hasn't already been committed to the record many times over? The Shark's 23 trips to Augusta National yielded three runner-up finishes, three other third-place finishes, and three more top-tens just for good measure. The most painful near-miss of the lot? 1996. Without doubt. Taking a six-shot lead into the final round, you could have forgiven the tailors for prepping the Green Jacket for him on the Saturday night. However, in rather painful fashion, the Australian laboured to a 78, turning a six-shot advantage into a five-shot defeat at the hands of playing partner Nick Faldo. At the time, the LIV Golf boss was acclaimed for the magnanimous manner with which he dealt with that sickening Sunday. "I just move through life and I don't let things affect me," he said in 2016. "You're going to have good and bad rounds and the indication of someone's character is shown on how you handle both."

Ernie Els

HOW DOES four-time major champion Els reflect on his 23 trips to the Masters? "It was a f***ing nightmare for the most part," he has said. "I won't ever miss the place. I've got a love-hate relationship with the place. It was always almost like a curse to me. It was not a romantic deal to me." The 'Big Easy' twice finished runner-up at Augusta: in 2000, when Vijay Singh beat him to the title; and 2004, when a final hole birdie from Phil Mickelson denied him a Green Jacket.

bunkered.co.uk › 43

Johnny Miller

MILLER'S RÉSUMÉ speaks for itself: two majors, 25 PGA Tour wins, the first player to shoot 63 in a major, two Ryder Cup appearances, a place in the World Golf Hall of Fame. Yet one thing that eluded him was Masters glory. That's not to say he didn't come close, however. On three occasions he finished runner-up, despite a bold prediction he made ahead of the 1974 event. "If I don't win, I'll be as surprised as anyone," he declared, adding that he wanted a Green Jacket "very, very badly". Alas, it wasn't to be, his runner-up finish in 1981 proving to be his last top-ten finish at Augusta National.

Nick Price

PRICE HAD a small period of domination in the golfing world, where he was considered the best player around and delivered by winning three majors in two years, including back-to-back wins at The Open and PGA Championship in 1994. However, most experts were left scratching their head at the fact that his best-ever finish at Augusta was fifth in 1986, despite the fact he became the first player to shoot 63 on the famed course that same year. Twenty starts yielded 11 top-25 finishes... but it could have been so much better.

Rory McIlroy

OH RORY. The Northern Irishman sure has put himself and his legions of fans through the wringer in this tournament. McIlroy should have pulled on the Green Jacket in 2011, but he blew up on the back nine and now Charl Schwartzel is forever a Masters champion. Since then, McIlroy has tried everything and practically manipulates his playing schedule around getting to Augusta with his game in the right shape. It's sort of worked, in that he has had seven top-tens in his last 11 appearances, but he still hasn't got over the line and into that blazer. Yet.

BEST PLAYERS **NEVER TO WIN**

Colin Montgomerie

FORGET THE BEST players to never win a Masters, Monty has a good claim for the best player to have never won a major full stop. But the Scot's record at Augusta is nothing to write home about, with more missed cuts (6) than top 20s (5) from his 15 starts and his best finish being a tie for 8th in 1998. The year before, ahead of a third-round pairing with leader Tiger Woods, whom Montgomerie trailed by three, he confidently declared: "I've got a lot more experience in major championships than he has, and hopefully I can prove that." Woods went on to win by 12 and beat Montgomerie by double that.

Hale Irwin

IRWIN WON a frankly ludicrous 83 times in his Hall of Fame career, including three US Open victories between 1974 and 1990 and a Champions Tour record that's only been bettered by Bernhard Langer. One suspects Irwin would swap that for just one of the German's two Green Jackets, though. His record at Augusta was exemplary, too, finishing T4, T4, T4, 5th and 8th in a five-year run from '74. He once said of playing the last nine holes of a Masters: "There's going to come at least one point when you want to throw yourself in the nearest trash can and disappear. You know you can't hide. It's like you're walking down the fairway naked." Quite.

David Duval

DOUBLE D has an Open Championship, a Players Championship and a Tour Championship on his impressive CV, but his inability to get the job done at Augusta has always been a thorn in the American's side. Duval, who spent 29 weeks at the top of the world rankings in 1999, has a peculiar record at Augusta, with finishes of T18, T2, T6, T3 and 2nd flanked by six missed cuts from 11 starts. He doesn't mince his words when it comes to his runner-ups, either: "Finishing second at the Masters is like getting kicked in the head."

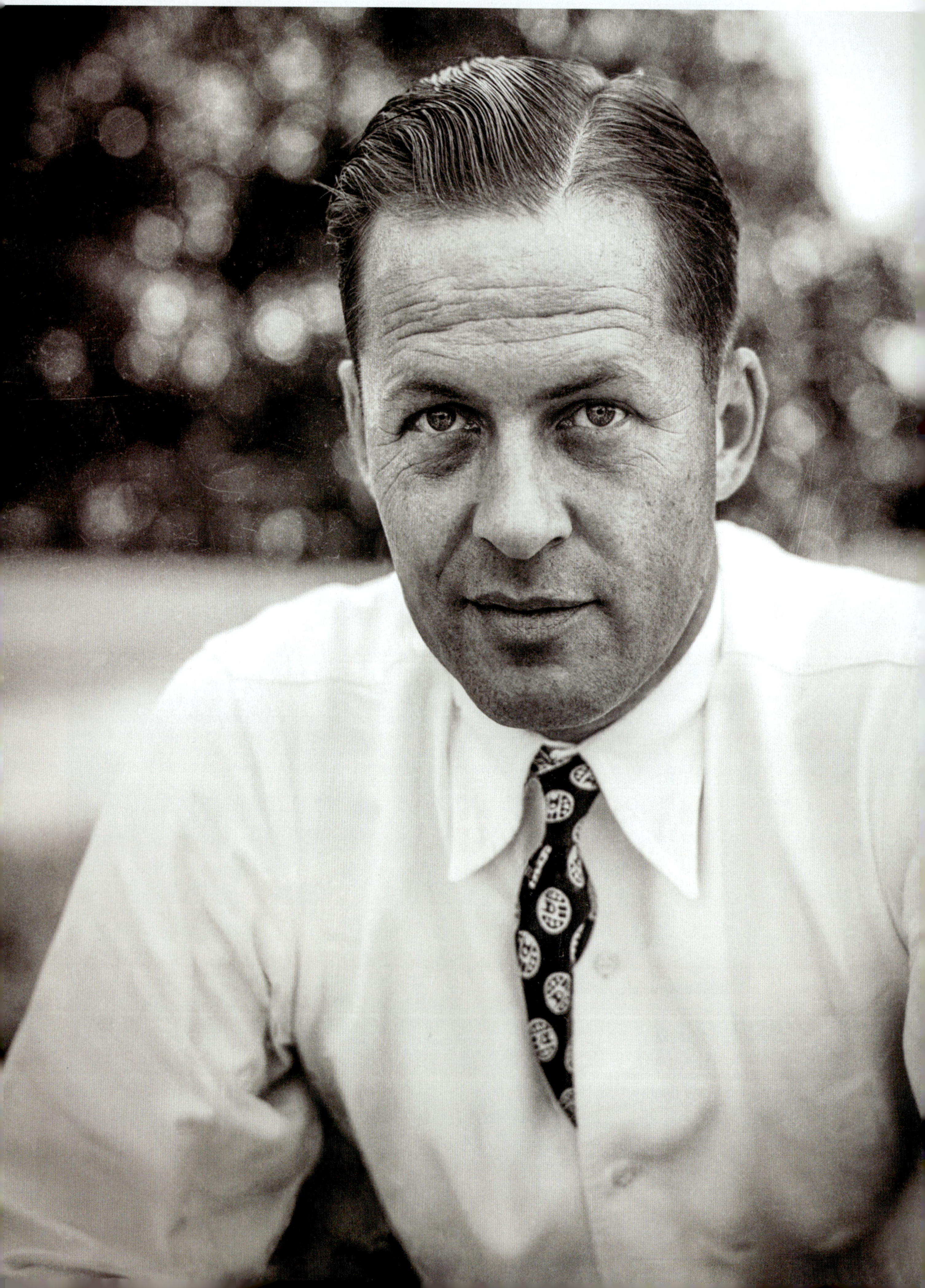

THE LEGEND

MISTER *Jones*

He was one of the finest to ever play the game and Bobby Jones' legacy will live on as the co-founder of Augusta National Golf Club and the Masters Tournament. We tracked down his grandson, Bob Jones IV, to better understand the man behind the icon.

WORDS **MICHAEL McEWAN**   PHOTOS **GETTY IMAGES**

*I*N 1966, A LITTLE UNDER six years before he died but with his health in sharp decline, the members of Augusta National passed a resolution to honour one of the club's founding fathers.

"It has been well and truly said," read the accompanying missive, "that every great institution is the lengthened shadow of a man. So it is with the Augusta National Golf Club: the man being Robert Tyre Jones."

Bobby, for short.

"He exemplifies the highest standards of sportsmanship and his position is pre-eminent throughout and beyond the golfing world," continued the edict. "Now, therefore, be it resolved that the by-laws be amended to provide for the position of President in Perpetuity as a lasting tribute… and he be the only person ever elected to that position."

To this day, the name of Bobby Jones continues to appear on the letterhead and masthead of the Augusta National Golf Club, his influence billowing through the dogwoods, trickling down Rae's Creek, and woven into each and every Green Jacket.

It is the mark of an icon that, more than half a century after his death, Jones' achievements continue to hold sway over what is arguably the world's most famous golf club. Incapacitated after a 20-plus year battle with syringomyelia – a disorder in which a cyst or cavity forms within the spinal cord causing, first, crippling pain and, later, paralysis – Jones died on December 18, 1971, after suffering an aneurysm. He was ready to go. Three days before he passed, he converted to Catholicism and was baptised on his deathbed by Monsignor John D. Stapleton, the rector of the Cathedral of Christ the King in Jones' hometown of Atlanta.

"If this is what it's like to die," he told the family members who had gathered by his bedside, "it's beautiful." Within an hour, he closed his eyes for the final time. Two days later, he was gone.

In that moment, the world lost an icon, a man who had both dominated and revolutionised the game of golf. Bob Jones IV? Well, he lost something far more important. He lost his grandfather. His 'Bub'.

Fourteen at the time of Bobby's passing, Bob is now 68. Like his famous ancestor, he too lives in Atlanta – just north of it, to be precise, in a town called Cumming – where he works as a licensed psychologist. "I have a general clinical practice," he says, "but I also work as a sports psychologist. I work with athletes in pretty much every sport. I love it."

His other great passion – quelle surprise – is golf. He's a member of three clubs: the Atlanta Athletic Club, which was his grandfather's home club; Sage Valley in South Carolina; and Highlands Country Club in North Carolina. Bobby hit the opening tee shot at the latter in 1928.

"They're all great," says Bob. "But home for me is the Athletic Club. Let's just say it's in the family."

Like many avid golfers, Bob says his handicap is prone to seasonal flux. In the middle of the year, when he's playing regularly, he's about a six but that can drift to as high as ten in the 'off' months.

Not bad, right? "Depends who you're comparing me to," he chuckles. Fair point. Bob's father, Robert Tyre Jones III, was a fantastic player who, at his peak, maintained a handicap of plus-three. As for his grandfather? Four US Opens, three Opens, five US Amateurs, a British Amateur Championship and a place in the World Golf Hall of Fame kind of tells its own story.

"I am living proof that the gene pool dilutes over time," Bob laughs.

As far back as he can remember, Bob knew of his famous stock but struggled to square his grandfather's reputation with the immobile, somewhat sad figure that so often sat before him.

"It wasn't until I was in my late teens that I finally saw one of his old instructional videos," he recalls. "I can still remember it as clearly as the day I watched it for the first time.

The character on screen opened his mouth and my grandfather's voice came out. That's when it really hit me that, 'Oh my gosh, that's

> **I play off anything between six and ten depending on the time of year. I'm living proof that the gene pool dilutes over time!**

HOME FROM HOME
Bobby Jones playing the Old Course in St Andrews, a course that had a huge impact on his career.

THE LEGEND **BOBBY JONES**

KEEPING UP WITH THE JONESES

Bobby & the auld grey toon

Bobby Jones had a unique relationship with St Andrews. In his own words, Bob explains it...

"I THINK MY GRANDFATHER'S relationship with St Andrews is, without question, one of the most unusual relationships you would ever see between a town and a foreign national. You know, this is a man who, when he first went there at the age of 19 in 1921, behaved so badly by withdrawing from The Open that Bernard Darwin wrote about him, 'Master Bobby is just a boy and a rather ordinary boy at that.' When he returned to play in The Open at Lytham in '26, his reception was less than warm but he still won the tournament. Something then happened over the next 12 months because when he won The Open at St Andrews in '27, he made the announcement from the steps of the R&A Clubhouse that he would be so honoured if the trophy would remain with his friends at the R&A. After that, the relationship between him and the town was cemented. He made another visit in 1936 on his way back from the Berlin Olympics. He said he couldn't be that close to St Andrews and not play there. Now, I don't know if you're ever looked at a map or not, but if you draw a line between Berlin and New York City, which is where the ship would have gone, it doesn't go anywhere near St Andrews. And yet he went and he played there. There were 200 people waiting for him at the first tee, and by the time he got out to the farthest point on the golf course, the entire town had closed up and come out to see him. Shopkeepers had put signs in their windows saying 'Shop Closed, Bobby's Back'. He returned again in 1958 when he was awarded the freedom of the town – only the second American ever to receive that honour, the first being Benjamin Franklin in 1759. He said two things in his speech during that visit that have always stuck with me. The first was, 'I could take out everything except my experiences at St Andrews and I would still have led a rich, full life.' And then he finished his speech by saying, 'With what you've done for me today, now I can feel as at home here officially as I have presumed to feel unofficially for years.' As he made his exit, a lone Scottish voice from the crowd began to sing, 'Will Ye No Come Back Again'. That's storybook stuff, isn't it? I mean, those kinds of things just don't happen. And yet to him – my grandfather – they did."

bunkered.co.uk > 49

him'. It completely blew my mind.

"We never talked much about golf and certainly not about his exploits in the game. He just wasn't one to talk about those things. But it was always on the TV at his home in Atlanta.

"I have many memories of sitting with him and my father and we'd watch the latest tour event together.

"Sometime later, when I was well into my adulthood, I realised I was quite critical of golf announcers on TV. I began to ask myself why that was. Finally, it dawned on me. When you grow up listening to Bobby Jones analyse the game and its best players, everybody else kind of pales into insignificance."

Just as it did for his grandfather, the Masters has played a big part in Bob's life. He estimates he has missed only two or three since he went for the first time in 1970. On multiple occasions, he has been stopped by a fellow patron who, upon reading the name on his badge, wants to know if he's related to the Bobby Jones. "It's always amusing to see their faces when I reply, 'Well, yes actually, he was my grandfather.'"

As well as being fun, many of these chance encounters have also made a profound impression on Bob, helping to both preserve and enrich the memories he has of his grandfather.

"I've lost count of the number of people who've told me what an impact he's had on them," he says. "That will never stop being wonderful to hear. How many people 120 years after their birth or 50 years after their death are remembered as vividly as he is, I wonder?

"He had such a great way with people. The late golf writer Alistair Cooke once remarked that one of the most amazing things about my grandfather was that he had an almost cat-like awareness of the person in the corner of a room who was being left out and that, when he talked to you, he made you feel like you were the most important person there. That's always stuck with me."

As well as attending the Masters, Bob has also had the opportunity to play Augusta National around seven or eight times.

"It's not fair to say it's the same place when my grandfather was alive but it's still a pretty special place."

His favourite hole on the property? It's not the one you might think. "It's always been the fifth," he nods. "People don't generally like

THE MASTER
Bobby Jones (left) and fellow Augusta National co-founder Clifford Roberts (right) look on as Arnold Palmer congratulates Jack Nicklaus on winning the first of his six Green Jackets at the 1963 Masters.

FOUR-MIDABLE
Left: Bob and wife Mimi at the Masters. Right: Bobby Jones with his 'Grand Slam' of major trophies.

THE LEGEND **BOBBY JONES**

bunkered.co.uk › 51

to go out to it because it's the farthest point from the clubhouse but, for me, it's one of the most strategically interesting holes on the course."

He pauses to correct himself. "I mean, it's a little less strategically interesting now since it had its makeover. You know, they changed the green complex a little bit and backed the tee up almost into another county but, other than that, I think it's just about the most interesting hole on the golf course."

'Makeover' feels like the perfect euphemism for the perpetual cycle of evolution within which Augusta National operates. The par-5 13th, for example, has been lengthened to accommodate the incredible distances the world's current best players are capable of hitting the ball. Land behind the hole's previous tee box was acquired from the neighbouring Augusta Country Club in 2017 and work soon began on pushing it further back up the slope.

Jones, of course, was a huge fan of the hole and the challenge it presented. Writing in his 1960 book *Golf Is My Game*, he articulated his belief that the second shot on the 13th should be "a momentous decision". "A player who dares the creek on either his first or second shot may very easily encounter a six or seven on this hole," he wrote. "Yet reward of successful, bold play is most enticing."

Advances in golf equipment and club technology have forced Augusta National Golf Club and its various chairmen to - very reluctantly - make changes to the hole to ensure that it retains as much of Jones' original intent as possible. The most recent tweaks, for example, resulted in the Masters tee being moved back by 35 yards in 2023. And whilst it's impossible to say for certain, Bob Jones believes his grandfather would approve of the alterations.

"I think 13 is a marvellous hole," he says. "I think it's still quite strategic. You know, the length that people are hitting the ball now, it does tend to take some of the strategy out of it. In the old days – and by that, I mean the 1960s – you were probably talking about hitting a driver and a long iron into that green. That's just not the case anymore. But what's amazing to me is, even allowing for the distance they can hit it, how many players still make bogey and worse on that hole."

Bobby Jones, it's worth remembering, didn't actually win the Masters. Together with Clifford Roberts and Dr Alister MacKenzie respectively, he co-founded the club and co-designed the course, but he never won the tournament for which Augusta National is most famous.

Indeed, by the time the first edition took place in 1934, Jones had long since retired. He stepped away from the game at 28 following his annus mirabilis in 1930, a year in which he completed his unprecedented 'Grand Slam', or 'Impregnable Quadrilateral' as the New York Sun's George Trevor so colourfully described it.

Roberts persuaded him to come out of retirement for the inaugural staging of what was initially called the 'Augusta National Invitation Tournament' but he could do no better than tie for 13th as Horton Smith took the title. As it so happened, that was Jones' best finish in 12 Masters appearances.

However, according to Bob, his grandfather's failure to win the Masters did not bother him.

"He was always very clear about the fact that golf was never an end in itself," he adds. "He always said that his family came first, his law practice came second, and golf was always third. It was for that reason that his stepping away at 28 made a tremendous sense. When you stop and think about it, what more could he have achieved? He never had any desire whatsoever to play professionally, so what more was there for him to accomplish? He'd gone to law school, had a young family. I think he was just ready to move on to the next chapter of his life."

Being the grandson of the great Bobby Jones has presented Bob with opportunities far beyond the imagination of most six-handicappers.

"I definitely am grateful," he says. "I've had the chance to play places that I would probably never have seen were it not for my grandfather.

"I've had the chance to meet people I would never have met otherwise.

"But the thing I always try to remember is that I don't get to do this stuff because I'm some great guy.

"I get to do it because of who he was. I frequently remind myself that I'm an ambassador for my family.

"I'm not the story, I'm just the ambassador."

> **I'm very grateful. I've had the chance to play places that I would probably never have seen were it not for my grandfather.**

BOBBY JONES
MINI BIO

Full name
Robert Tyre Jones Jnr
Date of birth
March 17, 1902
Birthplace
Atlanta, GA

BEST RESULTS IN MAJORS
Masters: T13 (1934)
PGA DNP
US Open Won (1923, 1926, 1929, 1930)
The Open Won (1926, 1927, 1930)
US Amateur Won (1924, 1925, 1927, 1928, 1930)
The Amateur Won (1930)

DID YOU KNOW?
Jones' four titles in the US Open remain tied for the most ever in that championship, along with Willie Anderson, Ben Hogan, and Jack Nicklaus. His five US Amateur wins are also a championship record.

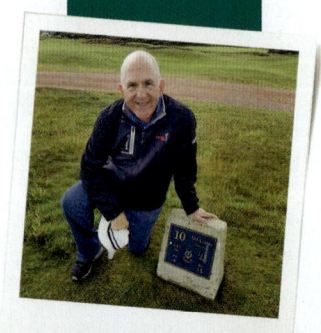

THE LEGEND **BOBBY JONES**

FAMILY AFFAIR
Left: Bob with his grandfather, Bobby Jones, and his father, Bobby Jones Jnr (or Robert Tyre Jones III). Bob's dad died a year after Bobby, suffering a heart attack at 47.
Below left: Bob and his wife Mimi at the Tour Championship at East Lake in their home town of Atlanta.
Below: Jones wears his Green Jacket during the 1949 Masters Tournament. He had played in the tournament for the final time the year before.

bunkered.co.uk › 53

The ultimate Hole-by-

THE MASTERS **HOLE BY HOLE**

Augusta National Hole course guide

A comprehensive rundown of all 18 holes at Augusta National, from records, to strategy, to historic changes

WORDS **MICHAEL McEWAN**   GRAPHICS **STEVE CURRAN & HEATHER ROWAN**

AMEN TO THAT
The spectacular Amen Corner, arguably the most famous three-hole stretch in golf.

1
Tea Olive

Par 4 Yards 445 Stroke Index 6

TIGER WOODS' THOUGHTS are illustrative of the challenge that awaits golfers on the opening hole. "If you are able to play the hole in 16 strokes [level par], you've picked up quite a lot on the field," the five-time champion has said. The tee shot is narrow and doglegs slightly from left to right, with a bank of trees framing the left and a large bunker guarding the right. Finding the fairway is crucial as your second shot needs to be precisely struck to find the right portion of a deceptively undulating green. Miss in the wrong spot and you'll have an extremely difficult two-putt to rescue par.

HOLE HISTORY

SCORING AVERAGE
Cumulative: **4.238**
Low year: **4.008** (1974)
High year: **4.474** (2007)

HIGHEST SCORE
9 Ernie Els, 2016

LOWEST SCORE
2 Frank Moore, 1940; Roberto De Vicenzo, 1968; Takaaki Kono, 1970; Scott Verplank, 1987; Retief Goosen, 2011.

HISTORIC CHANGES

1951
Bunker added at front-left of green. Underground piping of creek in front of tee.

1972
Masters tees relocated to the right.

1980
Masters tees lengthened.

2002
Masters tees moved back 20-25 yards. Fairway bunker reshaped and extended 10-15 yards towards the green. Portion of fairway landing area regraded.

2006
Masters tees moved back 15-20 yards. Trees added to the left side of the fairway.

2008
Ten yards added to the front of the Masters tees. Back of tees reduced to ease patron movement.

2009
Back of tee reduced seven yards. Tee marker relocated and Masters scorecard changed to 445.

2010
Practice putting green behind first tee reduced by 20 percent to improve patron flow.

THE MASTERS **HOLE BY HOLE**

HOLE HISTORY

SCORING AVERAGE
Cumulative: **4.775**
Low year: **4.467** (2020)
High year: **4.996** (1957)

HIGHEST SCORE
10 Sam Byrd, 1948; David Duval, 2006

LOWEST SCORE
2 Louis Oosthuizen, 2012

HISTORIC CHANGES

1946
Second bunker added to front of green.

1953
Green extended to the left.

1966
Right bunker at green reduced. Fairway bunker on left moved to the right in landing area.

1977
Masters tees rebuilt and moved approximately 20-25 feet to right adding 15 yards to the back of the tee. Bunker enlarged 12-15 feet on left side.

1996
Spectator mound moved back from rear of green.

1999
Masters tees moved back 20-25 yards. Fairway bunker shifted to the right.

2010
Front of green widened approximately eight feet.

2024
Masters tees moved back 10 yards and to the golfer's left.

2
Pink Dogwood

Par **5** Yards **585** Stroke Index **17**

IF YOU'RE GOING to contend for a Green Jacket, you need to take advantage of the par-5s, starting with Pink Dogwood. Never in the history of the Masters has the hole played at par or worse. In 2024, it lived up to its reputation as the second-easiest hole on the property, giving up seven eagles, 115 birdies and only 22 bogeys or worse. Right-handed golfers will look to sling the ball around the corner and down the hill. Stay out of the large greenside bunkers with your second and you'll give yourself a great look at birdie, eagle or, in the case of Louis Oosthuizen during the 2012 Masters, albatross.

HOLE HISTORY

SCORING AVERAGE
Cumulative: **4.076**
Low year: **3.885** (2011)
High year: **4.267** (1989)

HIGHEST SCORE
8 Douglas B. Clarke, 1980

LOWEST SCORE
2 16 occasions, most recently Morgan Hoffmann and Thongchai Jaidee, 2015

HISTORIC CHANGES
1953
Masters tees moved to the right.
1982
New fairway bunker complex constructed.

3
Flowering Peach

Par 4 Yards 350 Stroke Index 14

REPORTEDLY ARCHITECT Dr Alister MacKenzie's favourite hole on the golf course – hence why it has been changed less than any other – the third is a classic short par-4. Rule number one: stay out of the cluster of four fairway bunkers off the tee. That probably means leaving the driver in the bag and laying well back to give yourself a full shot in and the chance to better control your spin. Rule number two: it's better to be long than short, so don't get cute with your approach. The green slopes from right to left, with a thin neck on the left-hand side guarded by a bunker.

THE MASTERS **HOLE BY HOLE**

HOLE HISTORY

SCORING AVERAGE
Cumulative: **3.284**
Low year: **3.089** (2020)
High year: **3.497** (1956)

HIGHEST SCORE
8 Henrik Stenson, 2011

LOWEST SCORE
1 Jeff Sluman, 1992

HISTORIC CHANGES

1964
Masters tees relocated to right and rear.

2006
Masters tees moved back 30-35 yards.

Par 3 Yards 240 Stroke Index 3

THE FIRST OF the short holes is, in reality, anything but. Just ask Adam Scott. The 2013 Masters champion once admitted that he has considered laying up short of the fourth green when it gets particularly windy. The Aussie reasons that, if he makes bogey, he can "recover from that in a tournament". From your slightly elevated position back on the tee, the bunkers left and right of the green are in full and terrifying view. The objective is simple: stay out of the sand. Without doubt, this is a formidable test of club selection and your ability to flush your long irons.

4
Flowering Crab Apple

5 Magnolia

Par 4 Yards 495 Stroke Index 5

THE ADDITION of 40 yards after the 2018 Masters made the already-formidable fifth even tougher. The second longest par-4 on the course – only the 11th is longer – it was inspired by the iconic 'Road' hole on Bobby Jones' beloved Old Course at St Andrews. The first objective is staying out of the bunkers down the left. You will almost certainly cough up at least one shot if you wind up in them. Stay right of them and you'll open up a green that slopes from front to back. Just don't get too greedy on your approach, as there's an extra bunker waiting beyond the putting surface. A wildly underrated hole.

HOLE HISTORY

SCORING AVERAGE
Cumulative: **4.266**
Low year: **4.061** (2001)
High year: **4.475** (1956)

HIGHEST SCORE
8 Bill Campbell, 1957; Sam Parks, 1957; Chick Harbert, 1960; Jerry Barber, 1964

LOWEST SCORE
2 Art Wall, 1974; Scott Hoch, 1983; Curtis Strange, 1987; Jack Nicklaus, 1995 (first and third rounds); Colin Montgomerie, 2000; Gabriel Hjertstedt, 2000; Rich Beem, 2003; Russell Henley, 2017

HISTORIC CHANGES

1953
Masters tees extended forward 10 yards.

1956
Mound built at left of green.

1964
Fairway mounds added to right-front of green.

1967
Mound at left of green enlarged.

1972
Apron of green extended.

2003
Masters tees moved back. Fairway bunkers extended 80 yards towards the green. Fairway and bunkers shifted to the right increasing the dogleg. With the extended dogleg and movement of the tee, the hole was re-measured to 455 yards.

2010
Seven yards added to the front of the Masters tees without necessitating a change in length to the hole.

2019
Masters tees moved back 40 yards.

HOLE HISTORY

SCORING AVERAGE
Cumulative: **3.137**
Low year: **2.984** (1974)
High year: **3.269** (1946)

HIGHEST SCORE
7 Jose Maria Olazabal, 1991; Arnold Palmer, 1997; Branden Grace, 2016

LOWEST SCORE
1 Billy Joe Patton, 1954; Leland Gibson, 1954; Charles Coody, 1972; Chris DiMarco, 2004; Jamie Donaldson, 2013; Corey Conners, 2021

HISTORIC CHANGES
1959
Pond filled in at front of green.
1975
Masters tees rebuilt and widened.
2012
Masters and members tees connected to form a single teeing ground.

THE MASTERS **HOLE BY HOLE**

Par 3 Yards 180 Stroke Index 13

ANOTHER HUGELY underrated hole, this short beauty might also be the best viewing spot on the property. In addition to the sixth, you can also see all of the par-3 16th as well as the second shots into the 15th. From an elevated tee, you play towards one of the most challenging and deceptive green complexes on the course. It is split into two tiers. Your hopes of making par hinge on stopping your ball on the same level as the pin. If you don't, it's not going to be easy. Fun fact: there used to be a stream and then a pond short of the green, but it rarely came into play and so was turfed over in the late 1950s.

6
Juniper

HOLE HISTORY

SCORING AVERAGE
Cumulative: **4.157**
Low year: **3.986** (2001)
High year: **4.402** (1972)

HIGHEST SCORE
8 DeWitt Weaver, 1972; Richard L. Von Tacky Jr, 1981

LOWEST SCORE
2 17 occasions, most recently Keith Mitchell, 2019

HISTORIC CHANGES
1938
Green relocated and bunkers added.

1951
Masters tees extended forward. Green elevated. Bunkers added.

2002
Masters tees moved back 40-45 yards. Portion of fairway landing area regraded.

2006
Masters tees moved back 35-40 yards. Green re-grassed to create possible right-rear pin position. Trees added to the right and left side of the fairway.

2008
Six feet added to the left of the green. Left-rear bunker moved back.

2009
An additional ten yards was added to the front of the Masters tees without necessitating a change in length to the hole.

7
Pampas

Par 4 Yards 450 Stroke Index 10

NAMED AFTER its distinctive pampas grass, the seventh has undergone a raft of tweaks since the turn of the century to both lengthen and toughen it. However, the most significant change came way back in 1938 when two-time Masters champion Horton Smith suggested that, in order to add some much-needed character, the green be rebuilt and bunkers added. Staying out of the five sand traps that now encircle the putting surface is critical if you're going to have any chance of saving par. Accuracy off the tee is crucial, too. The fairway, whilst mostly straight, is extremely narrow.

THE MASTERS **HOLE BY HOLE**

HOLE HISTORY

SCORING AVERAGE
Cumulative: **4.819**
Low year: **4.628** (2019)
High year: **4.991** (1956)

HIGHEST SCORE
12 Frank Walsh, 1935

LOWEST SCORE
2 Bruce Devlin, 1967

HISTORIC CHANGES

1956
Green redesigned.

1957
Fairway bunker relocated to the right.

1964
Masters tees relocated to right and rear.

1979
Green restored to its original design.

2002
Masters tees moved back 15-20 yards and shifted to golfer's right 10 yards. Reshaped and nearly doubled the size of the fairway bunker.

Par 5 Yards 570 Stroke Index 15

THE SECOND of the par-5s and, once again, a terrific opportunity to pick up a shot or two. The statistics back that up. The eighth played as the easiest hole on the course during the 2024 Masters, yielding four eagles, 121 birdies and only 20 bogeys or worse. A big drive up the hill and to the left of the fairway bunker on the right will set up a blind approach into a long, narrow green that is bunkerless but guarded, instead, by a series of mounds. Incidentally, it was here, in 1967, that Bruce Devlin recorded just the second albatross in Masters history. He finished that year's tournament tied for 15th.

8

Yellow Jasmine

9
Carolina Cherry

Par 4 **Yards** 460 **Stroke Index** 12

THE FRONT nine signs off with a sublime par-4 that, much like the par-5 second, swings from right to left. Your tee shot needs to be drilled as far down the hill as possible to give you the best angle into a green that climbs steeply from the base of the fairway. No matter how precise you are with your drive, you'll still likely be hitting your approach from a downhill lie into an elevated green. The putting surface slopes from front to back and nothing good comes from being short. Any approach that's even a fraction off will roll all the way back down the slope. Deceptively difficult.

HOLE HISTORY

SCORING AVERAGE
Cumulative: **4.138**
Low year: **3.967** (2020)
High year: **4.401** (1955)

HIGHEST SCORE
8 Jack Selby, 1948; Richard Davies, 1963; Clay Ogden, 2006; Luke Donald, 2014

LOWEST SCORE
2 Earl Stewart Jr, 1954; Curtis Strange, 1980; Steve Jones, 1991; Danny Green, 2000; Bill Haas, 2013; Joaquin Niemann, 2022

HISTORIC CHANGES
1958
Mounding at right and rear of green built.
1972
Mound left of green enlarged.
1973
Tees split, relocating Masters tees 26 yards to right and rear.
2002
Masters tees moved back 25-30 yards.
2008
Right hole location softened on first and middle plateau.

HOLE HISTORY

SCORING AVERAGE
Cumulative: **4.299**
Low year: **4.082** (2018)
High year: **4.691** (1956)

HIGHEST SCORE
9 Danny Lee, 2009

LOWEST SCORE
2 Dick Metz, 1940; Doug Ford, 1960; Rick Fehr, 1987; Guy Yamamoto, 1995; Masashi 'Jumbo' Ozaki, 1999; Casey Wittenberg, 2004; Brandt Jobe, 2006; Robert Allenby, 2008; Charl Schwartzel, 2022; Gary Woodland, 2022

HISTORIC CHANGES

1937
Green relocated from fairway bottom to current location.

1968
Bunker to right of green enlarged. Pothole bunker right of green removed.

1972
Tees split and shifted left 10 yards.

2002
Masters tees moved back 5-10 yards and moved to the golfer's left five yards.

THE MASTERS HOLE BY HOLE

Par 4   Yards 495   Stroke Index 2

UNTIL 1935, the tenth was the first hole on the course – and what an opener! A long par-4, it plays sharply downhill and from right to left. A big, booming draw will open up the hole, but be careful to stay out of the massive fairway bunker that sits around 90 yards short of the green. Fun fact: the green used to be positioned to the right of that trap. However, in 1937, it was pushed back to the rise beyond the bunker. Not only did that make the hole much longer, it also made it much more difficult. The green itself slopes hard from right to left and is protected by a deep bunker short and right.

10
Camellia

11
White Dogwood

Par 4 Yards 520 Stroke Index 1

WELCOME TO the hardest hole on the course, the longest of the par-4s and the start of the glorious stretch known as 'Amen Corner'. (Technically, it begins with the approach into the 11th green.) A drive to the crest of the hill in the middle of the fairway is essential. From there, you have a lot to factor in: the elevation, the wind, the little pond to the front left of the green, the adrenaline of playing one of the most iconic shots in all of golf... Most players know that bailing out to the right of the green is the sensible approach. The received wisdom, indeed, is that if you hit the green, you've hooked it.

HOLE HISTORY

SCORING AVERAGE
Cumulative: **4.303**
Low year: **4.064** (1995)
High year: **4.644** (1956)

HIGHEST SCORE
9 Dow Finsterwald, 1952; Bo Wininger, 1958; William G. Moody III, 1980; Charles Howell III, 2006; Sandy Lyle, 2017

LOWEST SCORE
2 Jerry Barber, 1962; Brad Faxon, 2002; KJ Choi, 2004; Rory Sabbatini, 2006; Stephen Ames, 2008; Drew Kittleson, 2009

HISTORIC CHANGES

1950
Masters tees relocated. Pond left of green built. Green reshaped.

1953
Two small bunkers added at rear of green.

1990
Green rebuilt due to flood damage.

1999
Green, pond and bunker complex adjusted.

2002
Masters tees moved back 30-35 yards and moved five yards to golfer's right. Portion of fairway landing area recontoured.

2004
36 pine trees added to the right of the fairway.

2006
Masters tees moved back 10-15 yards. Trees added to the right side of the fairway and fairway shifted to the left.

2008
Several trees removed on right side of fairway and fairway widened.

2022
Masters tees moved back 15 yards and to the golfer's left. Fairway recontoured and several trees removed on right side.

THE MASTERS **HOLE BY HOLE**

HOLE HISTORY

SCORING AVERAGE
Cumulative: **3.270**
Low year: **3.030**
(2002)
High year: **3.548**
(1966)

HIGHEST SCORE
13 Tom Weiskopf, 1980

LOWEST SCORE
1 Claude Harmon, 1947; William Hyndman, 1959; Curtis Strange, 1988

HISTORIC CHANGES
1951
Green extended to right by 18 feet.
1958
Ben Hogan Bridge dedicated.
1960
Green raised.
1965
Tees revised to split level, side-by-side.

Par 3 Yards 155 Stroke Index 4

QUITE SIMPLY, the most iconic par-3 in the world. The shortest hole on the course, 'Golden Bell' is also probably the most famous and certainly the most photographed. A pure strike is required to carry Rae's Creek just short of the green. That, though, is easier said than done. The wind that swirls high between the tee and the putting surface is notoriously hard to gauge. Get it slightly wrong and you'll either be through the back of the wide but shallow green – where shrubs and sand await – or, worse, in the water. Countless players have seen their Masters hopes die on this hole. Golf nirvana.

12
Golden Bell

13 Azalea

Par 5 Yards 545 Stroke Index 18

AMEN CORNER draws to a close with, arguably, the best par-5 in golf. Players tee off from the most isolated part of the course – patrons are not permitted to go there – and have to draw their ball around the corner of a fairway that banks steeply from right to left. Water snakes up the left and across the front of the green, leaving golfers to contend with what Bobby Jones called "a momentous decision": go for the green in two and bring all of the risk (Rae's Creek, bunkers, shrubbery) into play; or lay up short of the water and leave yourself a tricky up and down for birdie? Iconic.

HOLE HISTORY

SCORING AVERAGE
Cumulative: **4.775**
Low year: **4.474** (2019)
High year: **5.042** (1976)

HIGHEST SCORE
13 Tommy Nakajima, 1978

LOWEST SCORE
2 Jeff Maggert, 1994

HISTORIC CHANGES

1954
Contours of green changed and bunker rearranged.

1958
Byron Nelson Bridge dedicated.

1967
Masters tees extended forward five yards.

1974
Masters tees extended to rear five yards.

1975
Masters tees extended to rear seven yards. Green rebuilt and recontoured.

1988
Swales to left and rear of green moderated.

1994
First permanent air system installed at green.

1995
Creek in front of green modified.

2002
Masters tees moved back 20-25 yards.

2010
Seven yards added to the front of the Masters tees without necessitating a change in length to the hole.

2023
Masters tees moved back 35 yards.

HOLE HISTORY

SCORING AVERAGE
Cumulative: **4.165**
Low year: **3.936** (2011)
High year: **4.413** (1949)

HIGHEST SCORE
8 Nick Price, 1993

LOWEST SCORE
2 20 times, most recently Martin Kaymer, 2016

HISTORIC CHANGES

1952
Bunker at right of fairway in landing area removed.

1972
Masters tees relocated to left and reshaped. Apron on green extended.

1974
Tees split.

1987
Green modified to provide for back left hole location.

2002
Masters tees moved back 30-35 yards.

THE MASTERS **HOLE BY HOLE**

14
Chinese Fir

Par 4 Yards 440 Stroke Index 8

THE ONLY hole on the golf course without a single bunker, and the only one in a six-hole stretch from 11 to 16 that doesn't have water, only a complete fool would underestimate the challenge of 'Chinese Fir'. Hitting the fairway is essential because the green is utterly treacherous. To begin with, there's a false front that will send any ball that comes up a whisker short rolling all the back down the hill. And that's to say nothing of the significant contours up on the surface itself that bank sharply from left to right. Par is always a good result ahead of two big birdie opportunities…

HOLE HISTORY

SCORING AVERAGE
Cumulative: **4.776**
Low year: **4.505** (1991)
High year: **5.097** (1998)

HIGHEST SCORE
13 Sergio Garcia, 2018

LOWEST SCORE
2 Gene Sarazen, 1935

HISTORIC CHANGES

1955
Gene Sarazen Bridge dedicated.

1957
Bunker added to front-right of green.

1961
Pond in front of green enlarged.

1963
Mound at rear of green removed and mound on right extended.

1964
Bunker at right of green enlarged.

1969
Tees split, moving Masters tees to rear and right. Mounds added in fairway on right side.

1999
Fairway mounds reduced, and pine trees added to right and left.

2006
Masters tees moved back 25-30 yards and shifted approximately 20 yards to the golfer's left.

2009
Eight to nine yards added to front of the Masters tees. No change to yardage.

2022
Masters tees moved back 20 yards and fairway recontoured.

15
Firethorn

Par 5   Yards 550   Stroke Index 16

THE FINAL par-5 is, much like the 13th, a classic 'risk and reward' hole. Favouring the right-hand side of the fairway off the tee gives you a legitimate chance to go for the green in two... but should you? A pond lurks at the front of the extremely narrow putting surface, making it hard to stop your ball if you do go at it. There's also a bunker to contend with to the right of the green and forget about going long. The green slopes towards the water. Trouble is, if you do lay up, you'll have a wedge into the green, and if you spin it just a fraction too much, you'll zip it back into – you guessed it – the water.

THE MASTERS **HOLE BY HOLE**

HOLE HISTORY

SCORING AVERAGE
Cumulative: **3.139**
Low year: **2.875** (2020)
High year: **3.422** (1950)

HIGHEST SCORE
11 Herman Barron, 1950

LOWEST SCORE
1 Ross Somerville, 1934; Willie Goggin, 1935; Ray Billows, 1940; John Dawson, 1949; Clive Clark, 1968; Corey Pavin, 1992; Raymond Floyd, 1996; Padraig Harrington, 2004; Kirk Triplett, 2004; Trevor Immelman, 2005; Ian Poulter, 2008; Ryan Moore, 2010; Nathan Green, 2010; Adam Scott, 2012; Bo Van Pelt, 2012; Shane Lowry, 2016; Davis Love III, 2016; Louis Oosthuizen, 2016; Matt Kuchar, 2017; Charley Hoffman, 2018; Justin Thomas, 2019; Bryson DeChambeau, 2019; Tommy Fleetwood, 2021; Stewart Cink, 2022

HISTORIC CHANGES

1946
New green constructed.

1947
Stream transformed into a pond. Green shifted to right. Masters tees moved left.

1961
Masters tees extended and relocated to the left.

1966
Neck of pond and left-rear of green filled in.

1973
Left section of pond filled in.

Par 3 Yards 170 Stroke Index 11

FROM THE last of the par-5s to the last of the par-3s, the 16th has been the scene of more holes-in-one than any other hole – in part because of the extremely generous pin position cut into the green on Masters Sunday. Be in no doubt: this a great spot to take in the drama if you're lucky enough to get a ticket. It plays entirely over water to a green that is protected by three bunkers: one short, one to the right, and a devilish one to the back left. The putting surface slopes dramatically from right to left, so you need to hit your shot in precisely the right spot to give yourself the best chance of birdie.

16
Redbud

17
Nandina

Par 4 Yards 440 Stroke Index 9

A DIFFICULT penultimate hole, the par-4 17th requires a precise tee shot to the crest of a hill in the middle of a fairway. From there, you'll get the best possible view of a green guarded by two deep bunkers. Hit the putting surface, two-putt for par, and move on. Incidentally, the 17th used to be home to the Eisenhower Tree, a loblolly pine named after the 34th president of the United States. Legend has it 'Ike' hit into the tree so often that he lobbied club officials to chop it down. They refused. However, an ice storm that blew through the course in 2014 resulted in its removal.

HOLE HISTORY

SCORING AVERAGE
Cumulative: **4.161**
Low year: **3.949** (1996)
High year: **4.348** (1951)

HIGHEST SCORE
7 19 times, most recently Fred Couples and Ted Potter Jr, 2013

LOWEST SCORE
2 Takaaki Kono, 1969; Tommy Nakajima, 1989; Davis Love III, 1998

HISTORIC CHANGES
1951
Ditch in front of tees removed and filled. Masters tees extended forward 10 yards.

1972
Tees separated, moving Masters tees back 10 yards.

1999
Masters tees moved back approximately 25 yards.

2006
Masters tees moved back 10-15 yards.

2014
Eisenhower Tree removed following historic ice storm.

THE MASTERS **HOLE BY HOLE**

HOLE HISTORY

SCORING AVERAGE
Cumulative: **4.230**
Low year: **4.014**
2001)
High year: **4.463**
1954)

HIGHEST SCORE
8 Denny Shute, 1959;
Homero Blancas,
1970; Masashi
'Jumbo' Ozaki,
1994; Ian Baker-
Finch, 1995; Arnold
Palmer, 2000; Camilo
Villegas, 2007;
Henrik Stenson,
2012; Jose Maria
Olazabal, 2022

LOWEST SCORE
2 Felice Torza, 1948;
Denis Hutchinson,
1962; Jim Colbert,
1974; John Huston,
1997; Chris DiMarco,
2006; Doug Ghim,
2018

HISTORIC CHANGES
1958
Mounding at left of green built.

1967
Double bunker constructed on left in fairway landing area.

2002
Masters tees moved back 55-60 yards and moved to the golfer's right five yards. Bunker complex adjusted, making bunkers approximately 10% larger. Trees added left of fairway bunkers.

2022
Thirteen yards added to the back of the Masters tees without necessitating a change in length to the hole.

Par 4 Yards 465 Stroke Index 7

AND SO it all comes down to this: one of the most famous finishing holes in the game. It's spectacularly good, too. Doglegging a little from left to right, a narrow tee shot – particularly from the Masters tees – needs to avoid the trees down the right-hand side and two large bunkers at the elbow of the dogleg down the left. Find the short grass and you'll leave yourself with a mid-iron approach to an elevated green where, again, there are two bunkers to contend with: one, short and left; the other, to the right. The putting surface itself is split across two tiers. A wonderful finish to a superlative course.

18
Holly

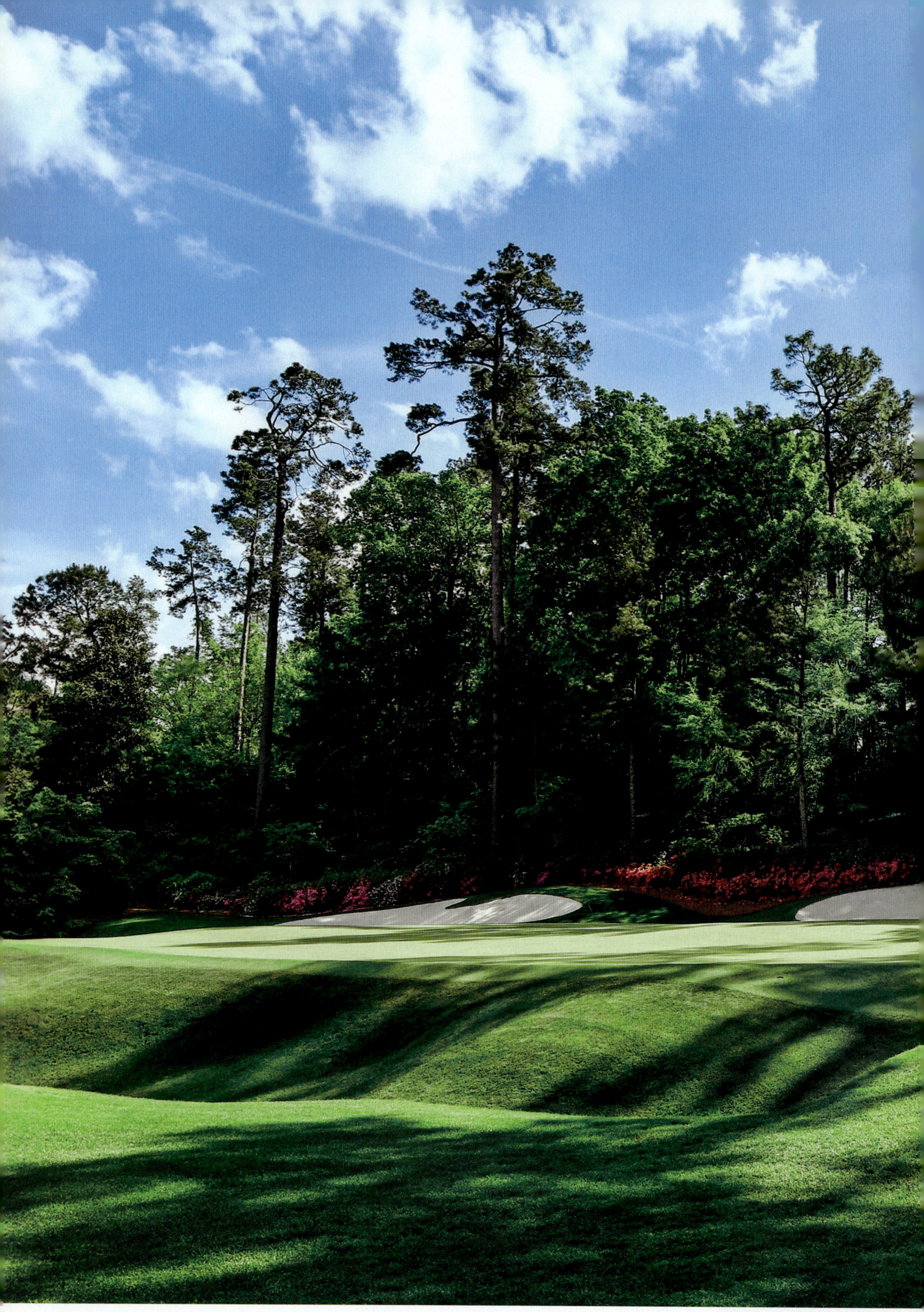

TRIVIA CORNER

50 THINGS
you never knew about the Masters

A half-century of facts, trivia and nuggets about the most intriguing major championship of them all

01
THE PERMANENT Masters Trophy, which depicts the clubhouse, was introduced in 1961. It was made in England and consists of over 900 pieces of silver. The trophy rests on a pedestal, with bands of silver provide space to engrave the names of each winner and runner-up.

02
THE UNMISTAKABLE Augusta theme tune was introduced by CBS In 1981. Simply called 'Augusta', it was written and performed by award-winning singer and songwriter Dave Loggins who was inspired by a visit to the club in 1980.

03
THE PAR-3 Contest first took place in 1960, Sam Snead running out the winner. There have subsequently been 100 holes-in-one made in the tournament and 21 sudden-death playoffs. Jimmy Walker holds the course record of 29, which he set in 2016.

04
AS FOR the main course record, that's shared by Nick Price and Greg Norman, each having posted a 63. Price was the first to do so, in the third round in 1986, with Norman's coming in the first round in 1996.

05
CHARLES KUNKLE holds the dubious distinctions of the worst official 18-hole and 72-hole scores in Masters history. The self-taught Pennsylvanian closed with a 95 in 1956 to compound a miserable week. He had earlier posted rounds of

06
RAE'S CREEK is named after John Rae, an Irishman immigrant who moved to Augusta in 1734 and lived just southeast of the creek's confluence with the Savannah River. He opened a grist mill in 1765 and died in 1789.

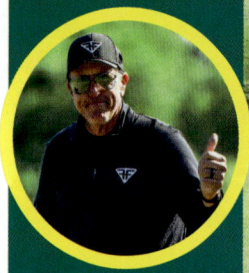

07
PHIL MICKELSON overtook Tiger Woods as the tournament's Career Money List leader in 2024. Lefty has made $9,781,117 from 30 appearances at Augusta – an average of $326,037 per Masters. Woods has banked $9,619,569 from 25 starts, followed by Jordan Spieth, who has made $6,015,822 from ten. Jon Rahm is the only other player to have broken through the $5 million mark at the Masters, with $5,063,017 earned from just seven starts.

50 THINGS YOU NEVER KNEW

78, 82 and 85 for a total of 340 – 52-over-par. It was the final year before Augusta instituted a cut. Today, players have the option to not officially record their score if they shoot higher than 95, as Billy Casper did when he scored 106 at the age of 73 in 2005.

09

NOBODY has broken 70 more often in the Masters than Jack Nicklaus, who did so an incredible 39 times. That represents 23.9% of his total rounds. The six-time champion also holds the record for most birdies (506) and most eagles (24).

10

A TOTAL of 41 different countries have been represented in the Masters, including Costa Rica, Namibia, Finland, Peru and Paraguay. The most recent country represented was, thanks to Adrian Meronk, Poland in 2023. The record for the most countries represented in a single Masters was 24 in 2015.

11

GARY PLAYER has hit the most shots in Masters history. The three-time champion struck a combined 12,061 shots in his 52 appearances at Augusta. That's 328 more than his closest challenger, Jack Nicklaus.

08

THE AUGUSTA National clubhouse was constructed in 1854 by the owner of the then indigo plantation, Dennis Redmond. It was later used as the home of Baron Berckmans and is believed to be the first cement house constructed in the South.

12

JUST FOUR PLAYERS in Masters history have recorded the same score in all four rounds. Walter Hagen shot 76-76-76-76 in 1939 and Lew Worsham shot 74-74-74-74 in 1954, Kenny Knox returned four rounds of 75 in 1987, as did George Archer two years later.

bunkered.co.uk ▸ 77

13

THERE are three named bridges at Augusta National: the Hogan Bridge to the 12th green; the Nelson Bridge to the 13th green; and the Sarazen Bridge to the 15th green.

14

ONLY THREE players have ever won the Masters on their tournament debut: Horton Smith, who won the first edition in 1934; Gene Sarazen, who succeeded Smith as champion in 1935; and Fuzzy Zoeller, in 1979.

15

ELEVEN Masters champions have missed the cut while attempting to defend the Green Jacket. Sergio Garcia, in 2018, is the most recent of those. And he did it in style, too, with an octuple-bogey 13 on 15.

16

THE 1969 champion George Archer has the curious honour of being the tallest man ever to slip on a Green Jacket. The Californian was a lanky 6'5". The shortest? Ian Woosnam. The 5'4" Welshman prevailed in 1991.

17

TOM WEISKOPF holds the record for most runner-up finishes without a victory. The 1973 Open champion finished second at Augusta National four times: 1969, 1972, 1974, 1975.

18

AT 14 YEARS of age, Chinese amateur Tianlang Guan became the youngest player ever to take part in the Masters when he contested the 2013 edition of the tournament. Ryo Ishikawa set the record for the youngest professional to feature when, at the age of 17, he played in 2009. Gary Player is the oldest player ever to have teed it up. He was 73 when he made the last of his 52 appearances in 2009.

78 ‹ bunkered.co.uk

50 THINGS **YOU NEVER KNEW**

19

ONLY FOUR players have ever recorded an albatross in Masters history.

Gene Sarazen
1935, 4th round
4-wood, 235 yards

Bruce Devlin
1967, 1st round
4-wood, 248 yards

Jeff Maggert
1994, 4th round
3-iron, 222 yards

Louis Oosthuizen
2012, 4th round
4-iron, 253 yards

20

THE MASTERS has been decided by a play-off on 17 different occasions. Sir Nick Faldo is the only player to have won in extra holes multiple times, while Ben Hogan is the only golfer to have lost in a play-off more than once.

21

CRAIG AND KEVIN STADLER made history in 2014 when they became the first and, to date, only father and son to play in the same Masters. A total of 18 sets of brothers have played in the same tournament, most recently Edoardo and Francesco Molinari in 2012.

22

THERE HAVE been 34 holes-in-one in Masters history. The most popular hole to ace, by far, has been the 16th, which has seen 24. The 6th is next, with six, while the iconic 12th, has seen only three: Claude Harmon (1947, 7-iron), amateur William Hyndman (1959, 6-iron), and Curtis Strange (1988, 7-iron). Jeff Sluman, in 1992, has the only ace at the 4th.

23

THE FIRST player to have a hole-in-one at the Masters was a London-born Canadian amateur Ross Somerville, using a mashie-niblick to ace the 16th in the very first year of the tournament. The most recent was Stewart Cink at the same hole in 2022.

24

WHILE WE'RE on the subject, there have been 107 holes-in-one in the Par-3 Contest. Gary Player – who else? – has the most with four.

25

JACK NICKLAUS holds the record for most birdies and most eagles at the Masters, with 506 and 24 respectively. Dustin Johnson had a record three in one round in 2015, at holes 2, 8 and 15. Johnson (13 and 14 in 2009) is also one of just four players to have ever carded eagles on consecutive holes, along with Dan Pohl (13 and 14 in 1982), Phil Mickelson (13 and 14 in 2010) and Webb Simpson (7 and 8 in 2018).

bunkered.co.uk

26

WHAT DO Henry Picard, Gary Player, Tommy Aaron and Seve Ballesteros have in common? They are the only players ever to win the Masters on a Monday.

27

GAY BREWER missed his title defence in 1973 after being admitted to hospital in Augusta with bleeding ulcers and a hernia the night before the first round.

28

THE 1983 Masters marked the first time in tournament history that players were allowed to use their own caddies, rather than Augusta employees. That year also marked the appearance of the first female caddie, when 1969 champion George Archer employed his 19-year-old daughter Elizabeth to carry his bag.

29

JACK NICKLAUS has recorded the most rounds under par, with 22, while Phil Mickelson is second with 19. Nicklaus, Tom Kite and Tom Watson are the only players to have recorded ten rounds in a row under par. Mickelson, though, leads the scoring average of those with 100+ rounds, with 71.30 to Nicklaus's 71.98.

30

CBS COMMENTATOR Jack Whitaker stirred controversy in 1966 when he referred to the gallery at the end of the 18-hole Monday play-off as a "mob". He was subsequently banned from the next five Masters for his outburst.

31

PRIZE MONEY at the Masters broke through the $1 million mark for the first time ever in 1988, with winner Sandy Lyle banking $183,800. In 2024, the purse was $20 million. For the inaugural Masters in 1934, the field competed for just $5,000, which works out to around $117,000 in today's rates.

32

THE BUTLER CABIN – venue for the CBS television broadcast – is one of ten cabins on the grounds of Augusta National. It was built in 1964 and is named after Thomas Butler, who was a club member at the time.

50 THINGS **YOU NEVER KNEW**

34

THE ICONIC driveway to the Augusta National clubhouse, Magnolia Lane is 330 yards long and is lined on each side with 61 magnolia trees, 122 in total. The trees date to the 1850s when they were planted by the Berckman family, who owned and operated the Fruitlands Nursery that sat on the land now occupied by Augusta National.

33

INTERESTINGLY, only six players have ever had a birdie on the final hole to win the Masters, the most recent being Phil Mickelson who did so in 2004.

35

SINCE THE inception of the Official World Golf Rankings in 1986, only five players have won the Masters while ranked No.1: Ian Woosnam (1991), Fred Couples (1992), Tiger Woods (2001 and 2002), Dustin Johnson (2020), and Scottie Scheffler (2022 and 2024).

36

CURTIS STRANGE, Corey Pavin and Ian Poulter share a rather peculiar feat: they have all recorded scores of 1-2-3-4 on a single hole during a single Masters. Strange on the 12th in 1988, and Pavin and Poulter on the 16th in 1992 and 2008 respectively.

37

GENE LITTLER and Tom Kite share the record for most Masters appearances without a victory. Both played in the tournament 26 times without ever slipping on a Green Jacket.

38

ONLY FOUR players have finished inside the top-five after turning 50: Jimmy Demaret, T5 in 1962; Sam Snead, T3 in 1963; Miguel Angel Jimenez, 4th in 2014; and Phil Mickelson, T2 in 2023.

39

GENE SARAZEN is the oldest man ever to have struck a ball at the Masters. The 1935 champion was 97 years of age when, as honorary starter, he hit the first shot of the 1999 tournament. He died the following month.

40

FRED COUPLES and Gary Player share the record for the most consecutive cuts made at Augusta National. Both registered 23-tournament streaks.

41

THE LARGEST field ever to take part in the Masters consisted of 109 players in 1962. The smallest, by comparison, is 42. That happened on two occasions: 1938 and 1942.

50 THINGS YOU NEVER KNEW

42
'AMEN CORNER', the name given to the part of the course that comprises the approach to the 11th, the entire 12th hole and the tee shot on the 13th, was coined by legendary sportswriter Herbert Warren Wind. Inspired by a song called "Shoutin' In That Amen Corner" by jazz singer Mildred Bailey, Wind used the term in a report for *Sports Illustrated* following Arnold Palmer's 1958 victory.

43
KEN VENTURI, a two-time runner-up at Augusta, holds the amateur Masters course record. He carded a 66 in the first round in 1956 – the first of the two times he finished second in the tournament.

44
SERGIO GARCIA has the "honour" of having made the most starts in the Masters before winning. His 2017 victory came at the 19th attempt.

45
THE MASTERS was first broadcast on TV in 1956. Ten years later, the first colour TV broadcast took place, with the first overseas TV broadcast coming in 1967 when the BBC showed it in the UK. Today, it is shown in more than 200 countries around the world, as well as on US army bases via the Armed Forced Radio and Television Service.

46
ANOTHER of the cabins, the Eisenhower Cabin, was built in the early 1950s following the election of club member Dwight D. Eisenhower as US president. It cost a reported $75,000 and was built to specifications provided to the club by the Secret Service.

47
TALKING of President Eisenhower, the former Commander-in-Chief had a run-in with club co-founder Clifford Roberts in 1956 after attempting to have a large pine tree to the left of the 17th fairway and 210 yards from the tee cut down. He had grown exasperated at hitting it so often. Eisenhower raised the motion at a Governors' Meeting only to be ruled out of order by Roberts who promptly adjourned the meeting. Hitherto known as the 'Eisenhower Tree', the pine remained a feature of the course until 2014 when it was destroyed by an ice storm.

48
IN 1975, Lee Elder became the first African-American to play in the Masters. He shot a 74 in round one and a 78 the next day to miss the cut. He would go on to play in the tournament five more times, with a best finish of T17 in 1979.

49
CLIFFORD ROBERTS, who co-founded Augusta National with Bobby Jones in 1932, committed suicide on the club's grounds on September 29, 1977. The then 83-year-old had been battling cancer and had recently suffered a debilitating stroke. He died from a self-inflicted gunshot wound on the banks of Ike's Pond, the body of water that features on final two holes of the Par-3 course. By coincidence, his mother also ended her own life by gunshot wound in 1913.

50
ANTHONY KIM holds the record for the most birdies carded in one round at Augusta National. The American had 11 (eleven!) en route to a second-round 65 in 209.

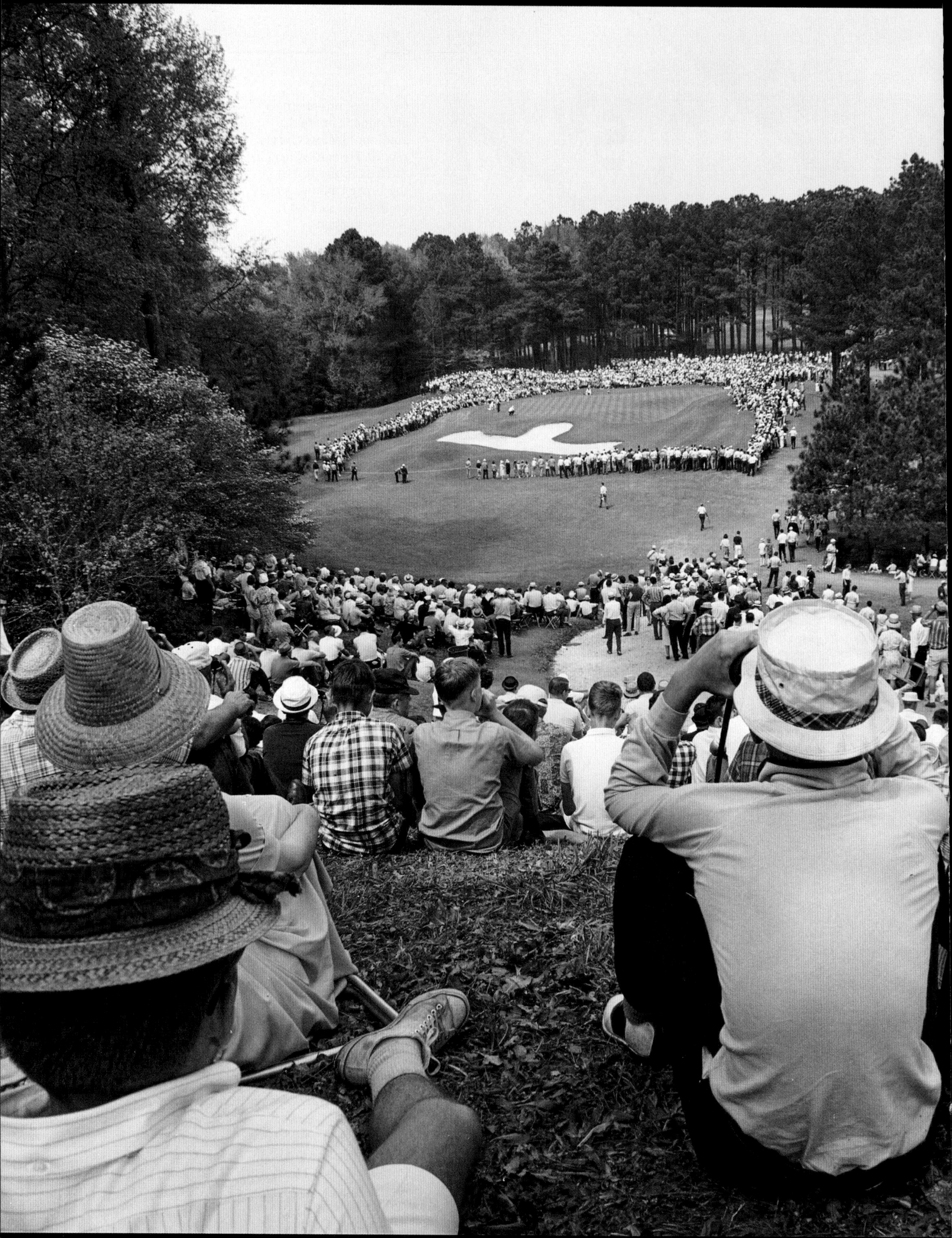

PHOTOS UNLIKE ANY OTHER

Augusta National in Black & White

These incredible archival images shine a fascinating light on how the Masters looked in the tournament's early days

WORDS **MICHAEL McEWAN**   PHOTOS **GETTY IMAGES**

TODAY, THE MASTERS is synonymous with bright, vibrant colours. However, there was a time when the only way for the majority of the world to consume it was through black and white photography and video.

Fortunately, many of those images in particular still exist courtesy of Augusta National Golf Club's archives, offering a wonderfully fascinating window into the early years of the tournament.

They show how the club and course have evolved in the near-century since they opened and how the Masters has become one of the most beloved, most iconic and most important tournaments in the sport of golf.

The next few pages are devoted to showcasing how everything looked in the days of black and white footage, from the course, to the players, the patrons, the media and even the traditions for which the Masters has become so internationally famous.

Sit back, relax and enjoy...

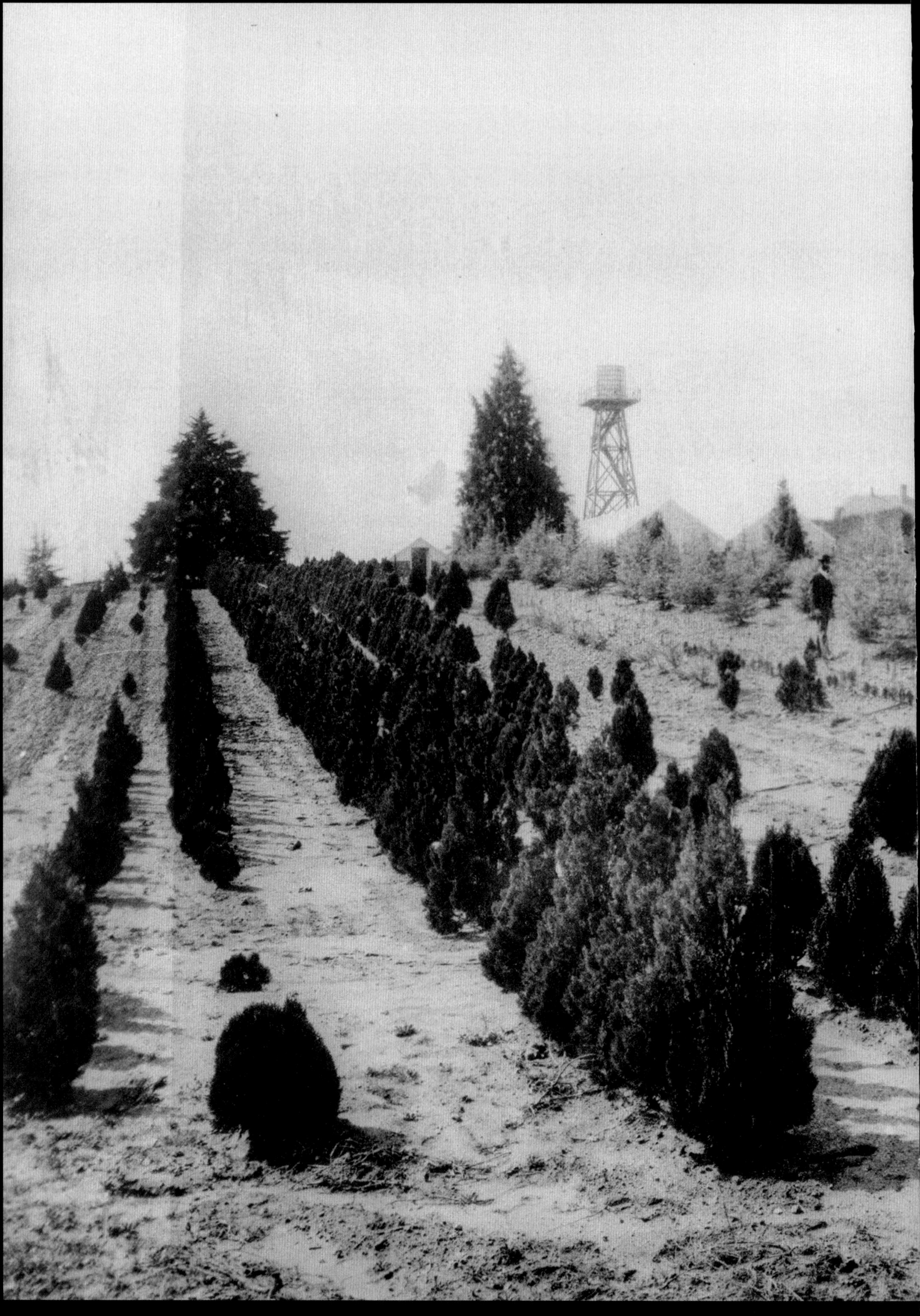

AUGUSTA NATIONAL IN **BLACK AND WHITE**

The Beginnings

Date: *July 1890*
Pic: *Augusta National / Getty Images*

The picture on the left is Augusta National before it was Augusta National. Prior to being purchased by a consortium of sorts – headed up by Bobby Jones – the land was home to Fruitland Nursery, owned by a Belgian horticulturalist called LEM Berckmans. The Berckmans family, *pictured above*, created one of the most important horticultural centres in the South. Fruitland Nursery, in fact, imported more than 40 varieties of azaleas and, quite literally, planted the seeds for many of Augusta National's most iconic features.

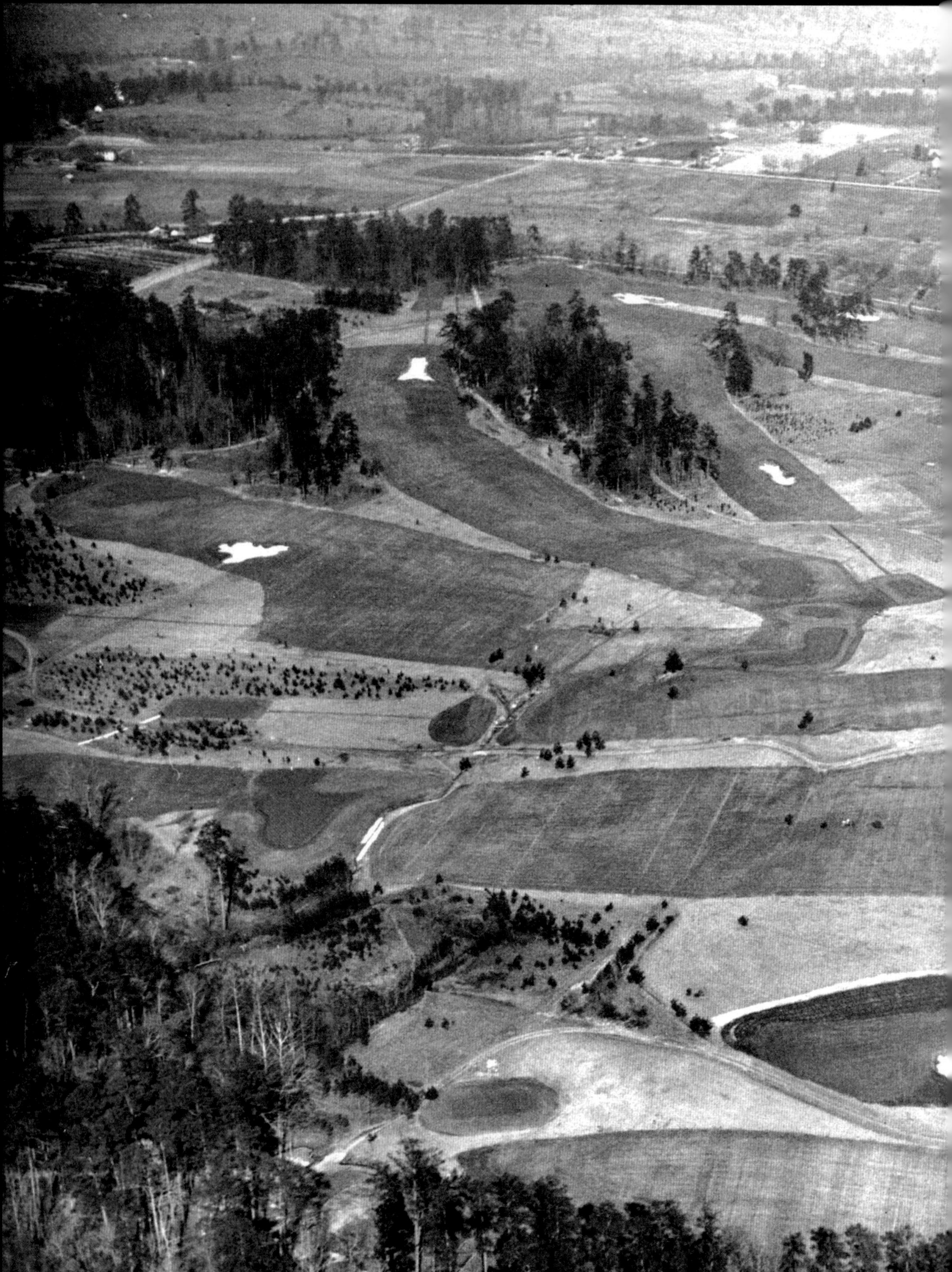

AUGUSTA NATIONAL IN **BLACK AND WHITE**

The Course

Date: *Jan 10, 1933*
Pic: *PhotoQuest/ Getty Images*

Designed by Bobby Jones and British golf course architect Dr Alister MacKenzie, work on the golf course began in early 1932. When it officially opened for play in January 1933, things got off to a slow start. During the first decade of the club's existence, a combination of the Great Depression and the club's remote location impacted membership numbers and finances, forcing Jones and co-owner Clifford Roberts to scrap plans for a ladies' course, squash and tennis courts, and various other projects. Pictured below is Magnolia Lane shortly prior to Jones and Roberts buying the site.

The Course

Date: Mar 22, 1934
Pic: Getty Images

The creation of Augusta National and, with it, the Augusta National Invitation Tournament in 1934, prompted Jones to briefly come out of retirement. Here he is crossing the bridge to the par-3 12th during that inaugural tournament with fellow player Paul Runyon close behind. In addition to the wooden bridge that has since been significantly upgraded, notice that the caddies aren't wearing white overalls. They didn't become a thing until the late 1940s. Also, for the first year of the tournament, the two nines played the opposite way around, so the 12th as we now know it was originally the third. The 13th, meanwhile, (then the fourth) is pictured above.

AUGUSTA NATIONAL IN **BLACK AND WHITE**

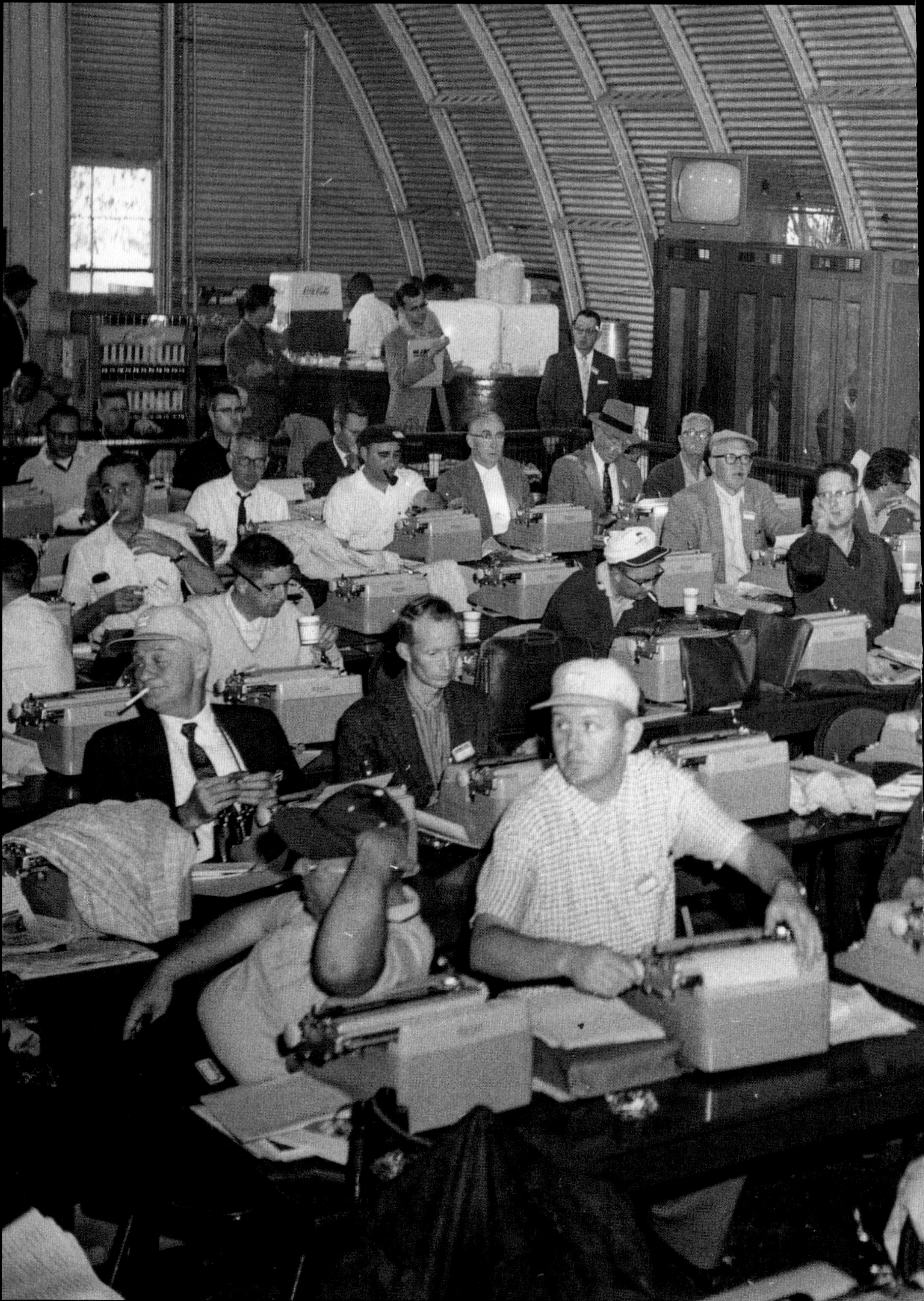

AUGUSTA NATIONAL IN **BLACK AND WHITE**

The Media

Date: *April 1953*
Pics: *Augusta National/Getty Images*

After originally operating out of the clubhouse and then a tent close to the first fairway, members of the press covering the Masters were moved into their own building in 1952. The so-called Quonset Hut, which you can see here, was used until 1990 when a new facility – four times the size – was opened in its place. In 2017, the current state-of-the-art Press Building opened for use. Rumoured to have cost more than $50m, the new media centre gives a nod to the old Quonset Hut in the Bartlett Lounge, a full service restaurant named after Charles Bartlett, one of the founding members of the Golf Writers Association of America.

The Patrons

Date: *April 1949*
Pic: *Augusta National/Getty Images*

The Masters doesn't have spectators; it has patrons. It is said that Clifford Roberts and Bobby Jones introduced the term, believing that attendees were not mere 'spectators' but 'consumers' of an experience. Augusta National Golf Club does not disclose exactly how many patrons attend the tournament but it is reckoned that up to 50,000 are on the grounds each day. Since the mid-1990s, a ticket lottery has been in operation with the odds of securing a brief for one of the tournament days reckoned to be as long as 200/1.

AUGUSTA NATIONAL IN **BLACK AND WHITE**

The Traditions

Date: April 1949
Pic: Augusta National/Getty Images

The Masters is renowned for its many famous traditions – which you can read more about elsewhere in this publication – but some no longer endure. One of those is the golf clinic put on by some of the players in the field. In the early years of the tournament, competitors would deliver short instruction sessions to the assembled patrons. Horton Smith, Claude Harmon, Herman Kaiser, Cary Middlecoff, and even Gene Sarazen and Ben Hogan all participated at various times. It took place on the Wednesday of tournament week until it was replaced by the Par-3 Contest in 1960. Three-time champion Sam Snead won the first edition of the Par-3 Contest. No player has won the Par-3 contest and the Masters in the same year.

AUGUSTA NATIONAL IN BLACK AND WHITE

Date: April 1959
Pic: Augusta National/Getty Images

Another sadly forgotten tradition is the annual Masters Parade. Inaugurated in 1957, Bobby Jones led the first parade down Broad Street in Augusta on Tuesday of tournament week as a flight of blimps from Glyno Naval Base in nearby Brunswick flew overhead. Just two years later, a crowd of more than 25,000 lined the streets of the Masters' hometown to catch a glimpse of the festivities. Marine corps bands, beauty queens, golf club twirling majorettes, and 150-foot balloons - all became beloved fixtures of the parade, which was favourably compared with the Macy's Christmas parade in New York City and the annual Rose Bowl Parade in California. Unfortunately, the fun was short-lived, the parade taking place for the last time in 1964.

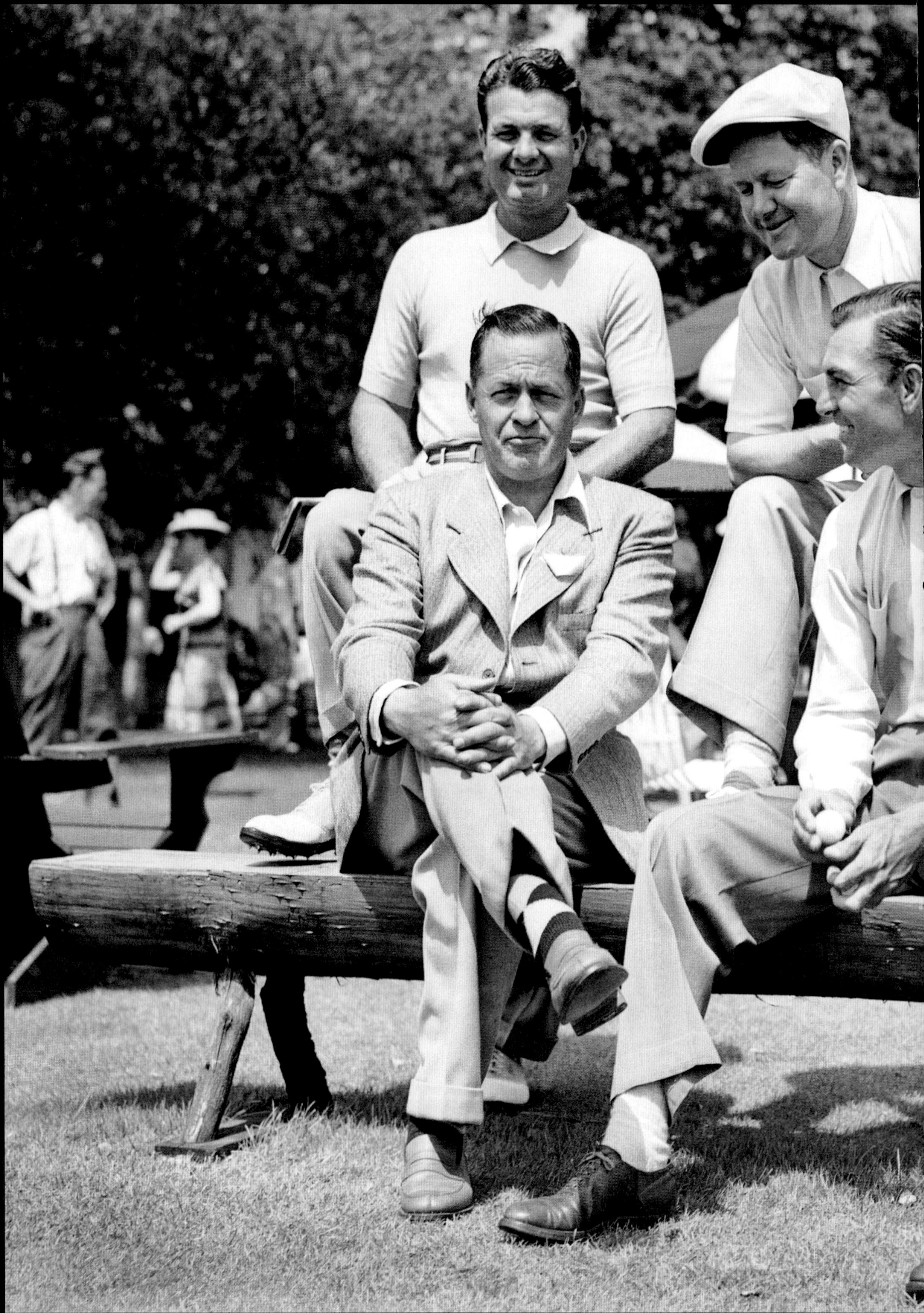

AUGUSTA NATIONAL IN **BLACK AND WHITE**

The Players

Date: *circa 1940*
Pic: *Augusta National/Getty Images*

Of the four men's major championships, The Masters is arguably the most difficult to qualify for. The tournament is by invitation only and has the smallest field of the game's marquee events. Typically, around 80 to 90 players take part – the largest the field has ever been was 110 in 1962. As of 2024, there have been 56 different winners, amongst them many of the game's greatest players, including the three gentlemen pictured here with Bobby Jones: in the back row Jimmy Demaret (winner in 1940, 1947 and 1950) and Byron Nelson (1937, 1942), and, sitting next to Jones, Ben Hogan (1951, 1953).

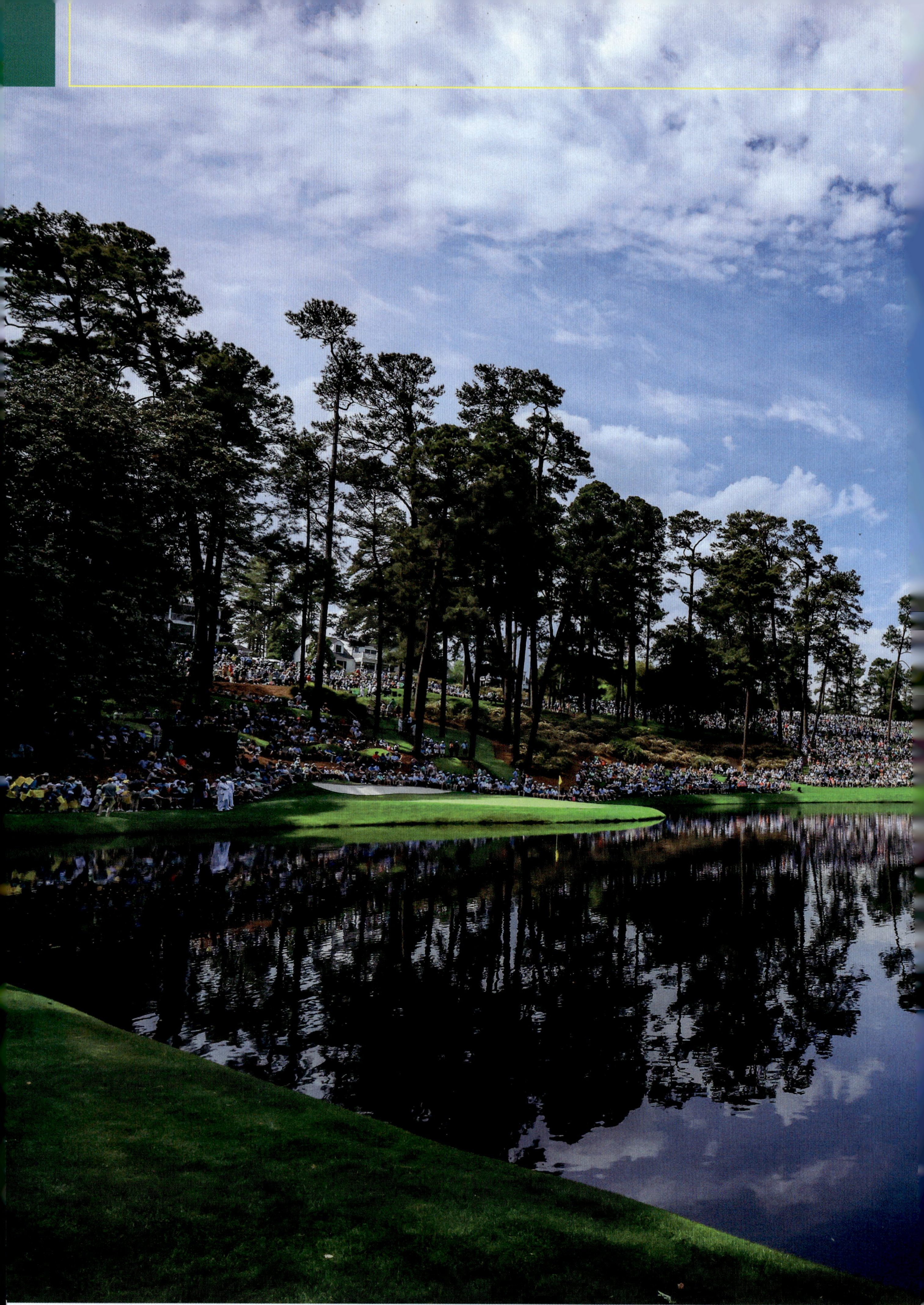

MASTERS TRADITIONS

TRADITIONS
unlike
any other

There aren't many events in any sport that do convention and heritage as well as the Masters. Alex Perry picks out a few of his favourite Augusta traditions...

PHOTOS **GETTY IMAGES**

Drive, Chip and Putt

THE DRIVE, Chip and Putt began in 2013 as a joint initiative between Augusta National, the USGA and PGA of America and sees 80 young golfers aged from seven to 15 from all over the world gather on America's most famous turf to drive, chip and, of course, putt their way into the Masters history books. It has quickly become incredibly popular as people get in the mood for the main event.

Amateur Dinner

WE ALL KNOW about the Champions Dinner – and there's more on that just a few pages from now – but the amateurs in the field also gather for their own meal, which takes place in the clubhouse on the Monday of Masters week. We presume they pick from the menu, though we quite like the idea of the previous year's Low Am choosing the food…

The Crow's Nest

SPEAKING of those not yet in the paid ranks, Augusta National pays homage to its co-founder and greatest-player-to-have-never-turned-pro Bobby Jones with a small apartment above the clubhouse in which the amateurs stay on the Monday following their dinner. It can only be accessed through a hidden door, but it's one room with six beds, so players tend to stay only one night.

MASTERS TRADITIONS

Par-3 Contest

THE ANNUAL Masters precursor that's now a family affair. The oohs and the aahs and the awws ring out around this corner of Georgia as tiny overall-clad offspring whiff tee shots with plastic drivers and smash putts ten feet past the hole. It wasn't always this way. There was a time when it was a chance for the patrons to watch that particular year's entrants fine-tune their game and show off their skills on the world's most famous short course. Legend has it PGA Tour star Ken Green was the first to have his children carry a couple of clubs each for the Par-3. In later years, now former Augusta chairman Billy Payne decided to embrace the changes and, among other things, the contest was televised for the first time shortly into his tenure. Fun fact: no player has ever won the Par-3 and the main tournament in the same year.

Honorary Starters

EACH MASTERS, around 15 minutes before the opening tee time, Jack Nicklaus, Gary Player and Tom Watson will make their way onto the packed first tee, crack a couple of jokes, then rip one down the middle to roars of approval. Starting with Jock Hutchison and Fred McLeod in 1963, the likes of Gene Sarazen, Byron Nelson, and Arnold Palmer have all played their part in this tradition, before Messrs Nicklaus, Player and Watson took over. It's a wonderful spectacle and an absolute 'must' should you be lucky enough to get your hands on opening day tickets for a Masters.

Skipping Balls

PROBABLY the most popular tradition among the fans, who congregate around the par-3 16th on practice days and goad players into attempting to skip their ball across the pond and onto the green. Balk at the challenge and you're likely to be greeted by a chorus of boos. Take it on and you'll be welcomed with open arms. Hole out – as Martin Kaymer, Vijay Singh and Jon Rahm all have in recent years – and you'll get as big a cheer as you will hear at any point in the week. It's tremendous fun.

Caddie Overalls

WHILE THE GREEN Jacket is the most recognisable item of clothing at Augusta National, the white boiler suits donned by the caddies are not far behind.

In the late 1940s, Augusta National co-founder Clifford Roberts, who served as the club's chairman until 1976, was concerned that there was nothing to distinguish caddies from anyone else – notably the gallery.

First, the club ordered caddies to wear a green cap with a yellow button in the middle. These days, that spot is reserved for the Masters logo.

Then came the rest of the attire. Initially, the caddies wore blue denim boiler suits – think farm workers from the time – before they were changed to white.

And that's how we know it today, though the original heavy herringbone material has been replaced with a modern and lighter cotton.

For almost 50 years, only caddies employed by Augusta could carry during the Masters. But while that tradition changed from the 1983 tournament, the boiler suit remained.

Veteran Augusta caddie Carl Jackson, who began working at Augusta in his early teens, said they "wore those uniforms to look uniform".

"I wore it with pride," he explained. "It was a uniform that showed you were a professional. Mr Roberts wanted everything to look the best that it could – the golf course, the players... and that included the caddies."

As for the green numbers on the left breast of each caddie suit, these are simply dished out based on the order in which players arrive at Augusta and complete their registration for the tournament.

The only number that cannot be taken is '1', which is reserved for that year's defending champion.

MASTERS TRADITIONS

The Big Oak Tree

TOWERING over Augusta's clubhouse is a giant oak tree dating back to the 1850s which, for one week a year at least, becomes a meeting point for anyone who's anyone in the golf industry. If you're lucky enough to get a Masters badge, this is a great place to "celeb spot" between golf shots.

Butler Cabin

THE TOURNAMENT concludes in Butler Cabin where the new champion is presented his prizes – notably the gold medal, Masters trophy and, of course, sport's most famous and iconic item of clothing.

If you're flicking through this publication in order, you should already have read all about the Green Jacket, but this made-for-TV event, hosted by the eminent Jim Nantz and featuring the new and previous champion as well as the low amateur and Augusta chairman Fred Ridley, is as must-see as the golf itself.

After the Green Jacket is presented to its latest owner, there is then a second running of proceedings on the nearby Terrace Putting Green for on-site patrons and officials, as well as a chance for the champion to pose for photos in their new threads.

bunkered.co.uk

FORE PLEASE!

The first 'Starters'

Introducing the Scots who began one of the Masters' most beloved traditions

WORDS **MICHAEL McEWAN**
PHOTOS **GETTY IMAGES**

THE FIRST 'STARTERS'

UNDER STARTER'S ORDERS
Scotland's Fred McLeod steps onto the first tee, supported by Augusta National chairman Clifford Roberts, during a 1970s Masters.

EVERY TRADITION STARTS some time, some place. Fred McLeod and Jock Hutchison could not possibly have known that they were pioneering of one of the Masters' most beloved customs when they hit the first shots at Augusta National in 1963.

Yet in its own way, in a sport besotted with its own reflection and at a tournament obsessive about pomp and ceremony, the Scots-born pair driving down 'Tea Olive' has become a significant thread in the fabric of both golf and the Masters.

These days, thousands gather in the early-dawn at Augusta National on the first Thursday of April to observe and be part of the 'Honorary Starters' ceremony. At 8.15am, Jack Nicklaus – a winner of the Green Jacket a record six times – is introduced to the crowd by club chairman Fred Ridley before firing a drive down the fairway. The swing is neither as fluid nor as powerful as it once was but nobody cares. This has nothing to do with form and everything to do with respect.

Gary Player, a three-time champion and the first non-American to win the tournament, follows. Invariably, he outdrives Jack, which he celebrates with the kind of high-kicking gusto you seldom see from a man of 84.

Then it's the turn of Tom Watson, an honorary starter since 2022, with his swing as elegant as it's always been.

With that, the first men's major of the year is underway and, as the trio retreat to the media centre where they hold court for the next hour or so, the serious business of trying to join them at the following year's Champions Dinner unfolds in earnest.

As conventions go, it's both harmless and perfectly pitched. A fuzzy-centred fusion of past and present that even the most cynical secretly enjoy.

Appropriately, Nicklaus won the first of his six Masters in the year this tradition began. Also that year, Horton Smith, the winner of the first and third Masters, passed away.

It's not quite clear why Smith wasn't given the honour of hitting the first shot in 1963. Despite being in the final few months of his long-standing

bunkered.co.uk 107

battle with Hodgkin's disease – a brave fight that had cost him a lung six years prior – he still played that year.

Instead, the privilege fell to McLeod and Hutchison, a pair of expatriated Scots.

Born in North Berwick in April 1882, McLeod joined the town's Bass Rock Golf Club at the age of seventeen. He enjoyed a considerable amount of success and, in 1903, followed the lead of many of his countrymen by emigrating to the US to try to establish himself as a professional.

Within weeks of his arrival, he entered his first major, the US Open at Baltusrol Golf Club in New Jersey. He finished in a tie for 26th as another North Berwick man, Willie Anderson, won for the second time. He to Jim Barnes in the second PGA Championship.

His contribution to the game was recognised with an invitation from the great Bobby Jones to play in the first edition of the Masters in 1934. He finished in a tie for 50th.

The following year, McLeod was joined at Augusta by Jock Hutchison.

Born in St Andrews in 1884, Hutchison was another of the Scottish contingent to head across the Atlantic in search of golfing fame and fortune in the early 1900s.

Having originally settled in Pittsburgh at the Allegheny Country Club, he moved on to Glen View in the Village of Golf, Illinois, in 1918. He became a PGA professional the following year and, the year after that, a US citizen.

> **As conventions go, it's perfectly harmless, a fuzzy-centred fusion of past and present that even the most cynical secretly enjoy.**

beat Musselburgh-born David Brown in a playoff, as Scottish golfers occupied the entire top-ten.

Five years after he made his debut, it was McLeod's turn to have his name engraved on the US Open trophy. He defeated Willie Smith in a play-off at Myopia Hunt in Massachusetts, setting a peculiar record in the process. At only five feet four inches tall and tipping the scales at just seven stone ten pounds at the end of the tournament, he was –and remains – the smallest man ever to claim the title.

His diminutive stature, allied to his killer instinct on the course, earned him the nickname 'The Wasp'. He justified the moniker time and again, winning the 1909 and 1920 North and South Opens at Pinehurst, the 1912 Shawnee Open, the 1924 St Petersburg Open and the 1927 Maryland Open. In 1919, he finished runner up

That was only the second most significant thing to happen to Hutchison in 1920. With three runner-up finishes already to his name, he finally won his first major, narrowly defeating James Douglas Elder in the final of the PGA Championship at the Flossmoor Country Club, just outside Chicago.

Ten months later, he returned to St Andrews where he became the first US-based golfer to win golf's oldest professional tournament.

'Jovial Jock' lived up to his reputation on his return to the US, singing the words to 'Sailing, Sailing' by Godfrey Marks as he led a group of eight Americans off the Carmania ocean liner whilst cradling the Claret Jug in his arms.

Together with Walter Hagen and Jim Barnes, Hutchison formed 'The American Triumvirate', so-called because of their

STARTING SOMETHING
Right, McLeod and Hutchison at the 1970s Masters doing their Honorary Starter duties and, below, with Augusta National co-founder Clifford Roberts.

108 ‹ bunkered.co.uk

THE FIRST 'STARTERS'

FORE, PLEASE!

Every honorary starter in Masters history

Jock Hutchison
1963-1973

Fred McLeod
1963-1976

Byron Nelson
1981-2001

Gene Sarazen
1981-1999

Ken Venturi
1983

Sam Snead
1984-2002

Arnold Palmer
2007-2016

Jack Nicklaus
2010-present

Gary Player
2012-present

Lee Elder
2021

Tom Watson
2022-present

ICONS
Left: Phil Harison, McLeod, Hutchison, and Gummy Harison at the 1969 Masters.

dominance of the game during the 1910s and 1920s.

Like McLeod, he found the going tough in the Masters, finishing in a tie for 51st on his debut in 1935. However, when Augusta staged the inaugural PGA Seniors' Championship in 1937, it was he who won. The following year, McLeod took the title.

In 1954, in honour of their respective contributions to the game, Augusta National invited the Scots-born duo to play a 'ceremonial' round at the start of the Masters before officially withdrawing from the tournament. They continued to do this until 1962 - playing sometimes 18, sometimes nine - before, in 1963, they were given a new, more formal role.

"As has been the tradition for years, two grand old champions will start the parade Thursday as the opening twosome," reported the Augusta Chronicle in 1963. The following year, the words 'Honorary Starter' were listed next to each of their names in the list of tee times.

"Leading off the Masters is the greatest honour we can have," said Hutchison in a 1963 interview. "I would rather do this than win a tournament."

He continued in the role until 1973, when his deteriorating health forced him to stand down. McLeod pressed on alone for the next three years, hitting the ceremonial opening drive for the final time on April 8, 1976, at the age of 93. He died precisely a month later.

Hutchison passed away in September 1977.

The honorary starter tradition was subsequently abandoned for a few years until its revival in 1981.

Since then, nine other golf greats have got the tournament underway. More will follow. For all that has gone before, it rather feels – appropriately enough – as though this particular tradition is just getting started.

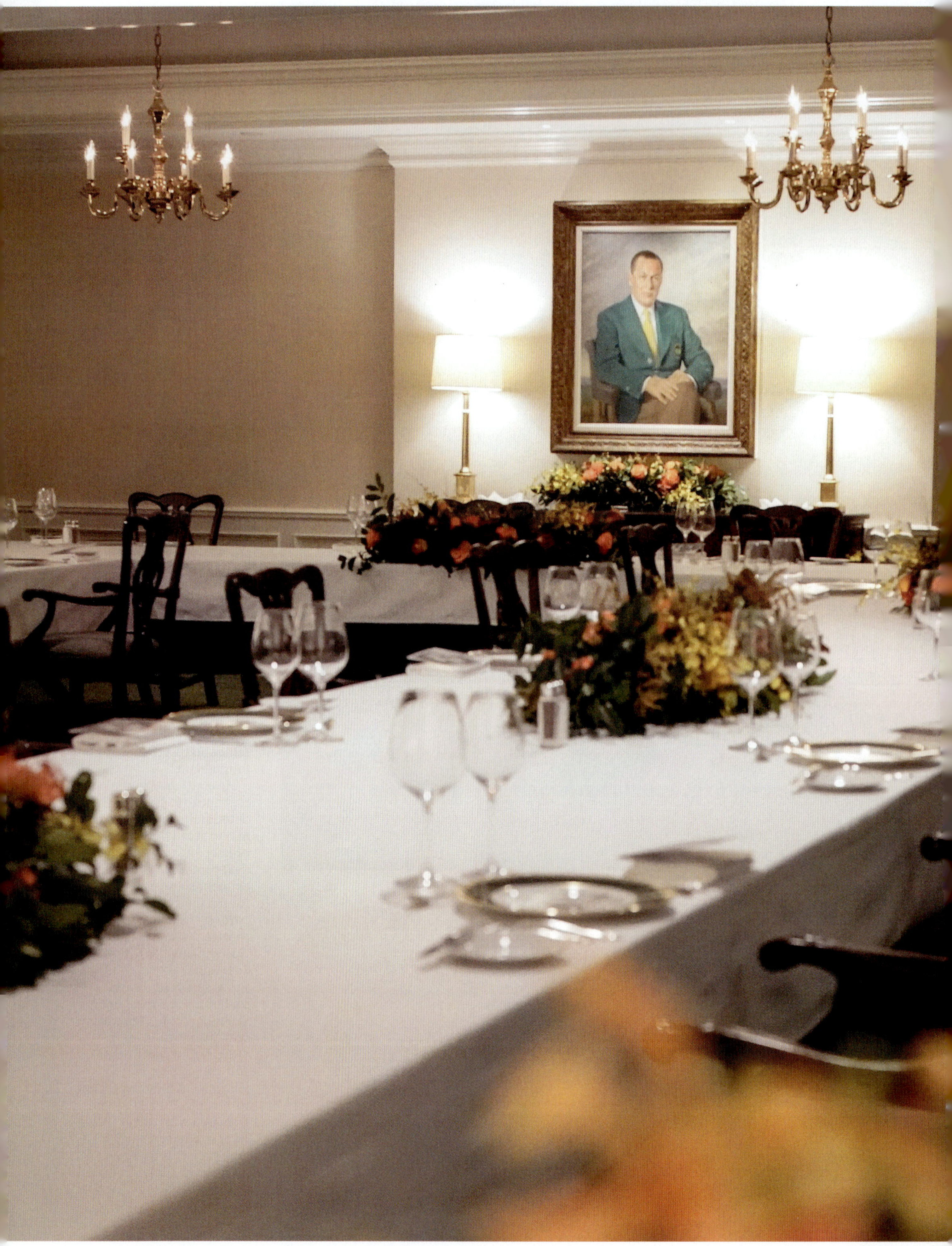

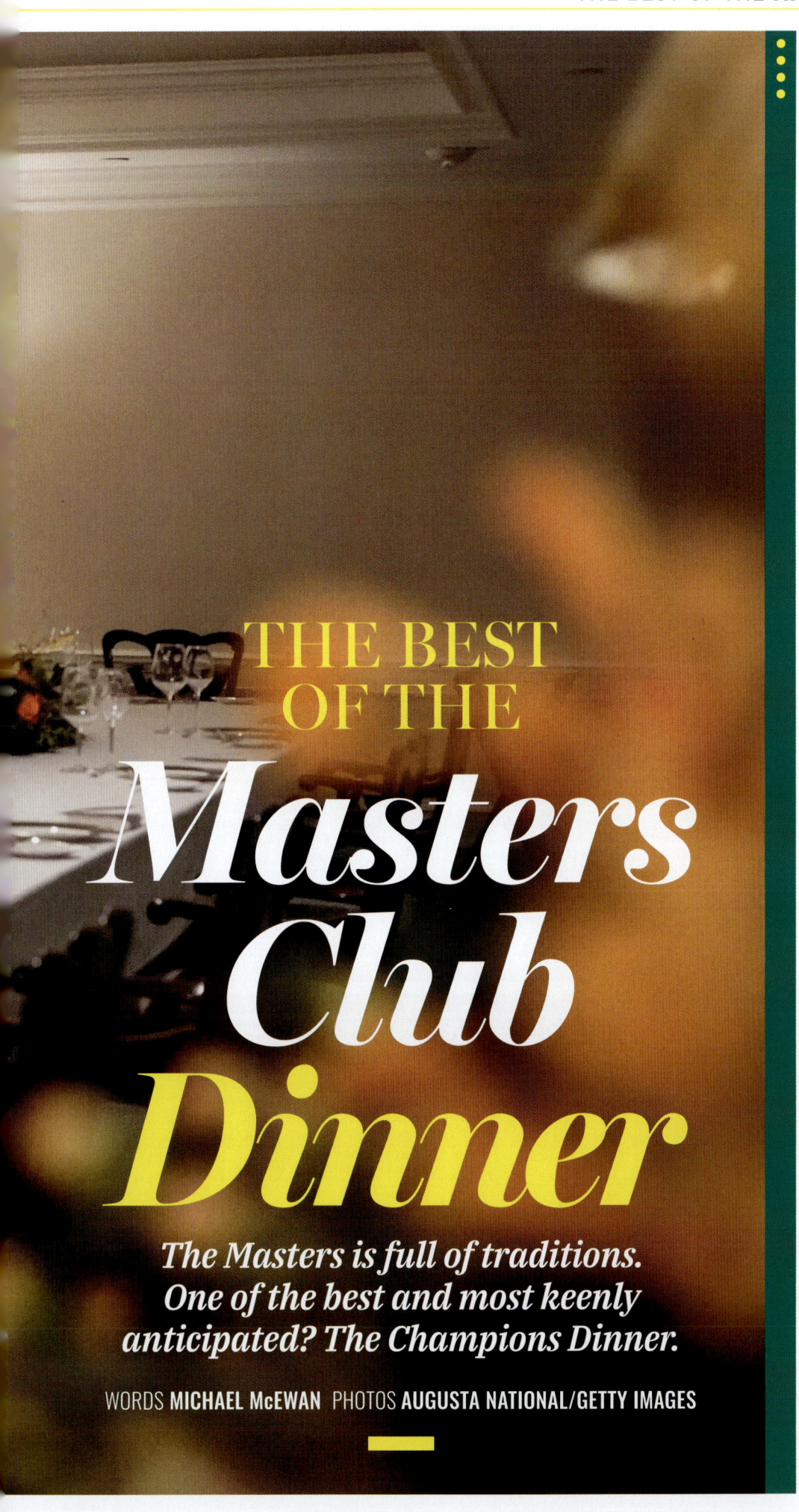

THE BEST OF THE **MASTERS CLUB DINNER**

The Best of the Masters Club Dinner

The Masters is full of traditions. One of the best and most keenly anticipated? The Champions Dinner.

WORDS **MICHAEL McEWAN** PHOTOS **AUGUSTA NATIONAL/GETTY IMAGES**

SINCE 1952, it has been customary for the winner of the previous year's tournament to set the menu for the so-called 'Masters Club' dinner, which is held on the Tuesday night of Masters week.

Sometimes known as the 'Champions Dinner', the tradition began when defending champion Ben Hogan organised a meal for all previous winners. Following the success of the night, the nine-time major champion proposed the formation of the Masters Club, with membership limited to the tournament's champions.

Honorary memberships were also extended to Augusta National co-founders Bobby Jones and Clifford Roberts, while subsequent chairmen of the golf club – Bill Lane, Hord Hardin, Jack Stephens, Hootie Johnson, Billy Payne and, most recently, Fred Ridley – have also been added as honorary members.

Each year, the defending champion selects the menu and acts as host for the evening. In return, they receive an inscribed gold locket in the form of the club emblem – a token of their membership of the Masters Club.

As you might expect, some people have got rather creative with their choices of food. Here are some of the most memorable menus that have been on offer, from the more traditional meals to the downright bizarre...

Bernhard Langer
(1986 & 1994)
It wasn't until the 1980s that Masters Club menus were first recorded, such was the simple, traditional fare customarily served at the dinner. German icon Langer was one of the first players to bring their own culture to the dinner, and many subsequent champions have followed suit. He chose Wiener schnitzel, which is breaded veal, and Black Forest cake, two popular meals in Germany. He won his second Green Jacket in 1993, and went with turkey for his main the following year.

bunkered.co.uk > 111

Sandy Lyle
(1989)

Those who attended the Champions Dinner in 1989 won't forget it in a hurry. Lyle made his country proud by serving up the classic Scottish dish of haggis, neeps and tatties. Not only that, he went the whole ten yards and attended the dinner in a kilt. "The older guys, like Jack Nicklaus, had been to Scotland and knew what haggis was but the newer ones, guys like Larry Mize, they weren't too sure about that," Lyle later told the *Augusta Chronicle*.

Tiger Woods
(1998)

Tiger's has to be the most famous Champions Dinner of all time. After winning his first major the previous year at the age of 21, Woods returned to Augusta National in 1998 where he served up cheeseburgers, fries and milkshakes. "Hey, it's part of being young" explained Woods. He has, of course, won the Masters on five occasions. He chose steak, chicken and sushi on his 2002 and 2003 menus; served fajitas in 2006; and went with prime steak and chicken fajitas in 2020.

Mike Weir
(2004)

Weir caused a bit of a shock by winning the 2003 Masters. To this day, the left-hander remains the only Canadian man to win a major championship. He caused a bit of a stir with his Champions Dinner menu, too, selecting some rather intriguing meats from his native country. Weir served up elk and wild boar, as well as Arctic chair (which is a type of fish) and a selection of Canadian beer, naturally.

Phil Mickelson
(2005, 2007 & 2011)

Mickelson finally won his first Masters title in 2004 and has since gone on to host three Champions Dinners in his time. For his first, he went Italian, serving lobster ravioli in tomato cream sauce, Caesar salad and garlic bread. In 2007, he treated the members to barbecued ribs, chicken, sausage and pulled pork. Most recently, in 2011, Mickelson provided a classy menu honouring Seve Ballesteros, who was too ill to attend. He served Spanish seafood paella, tortillas and Spanish apple pie. "I just want him to know we all wish he was here and we are thinking about him," Phil explained.

Zach Johnson
(2008)

Johnson crammed as many dishes and items of food as possible into his menu. The headline dish was veal osso bucco ravioli, which the menu indicated was the main course. However, Johnson, perhaps thinking he might not have

112 ‹ bunkered.co.uk

THE BEST OF THE MASTERS CLUB DINNER

DINNER IS SERVED
Top: the assembled champions for Jon Rahm's dinner in April 2023; Far left: Tiger Woods' menu from 2020; Left: the table setting for the event.

the opportunity again, also provided his fellow champs with jumbo shrimp, crab cakes, lobster bisque, filet mignon, seared ahi tuna, Iowa corn pudding, sweet potato casserole, and flourless chocolate cake.

Adam Scott
(2014)
Scott served up one of the more unusual menus at Augusta. He asked for his favourite dish to be flown in from Australia, as he believed he had to go all-out to impress the members present. That included Moreton Bay 'bugs', which were in fact just baby lobsters. Scott's appetiser was an artichoke and arugula salad with calamari, the main comprised Australian Wagyu beef New York Strip steak, served with the lobster, and strawberry and passion fruit pavlova for dessert, served with Anzac biscuit and vanilla sundae.

Danny Willett
(2017)
After his shock win in 2016, English ace Willett stayed true to his Yorkshire roots with his menu at the Champions Dinner the following year. He served a classic Sunday roast of prime rib beef, with roast potatoes, vegetables, and Yorkshire puddings. That was followed by an apple crumble with vanilla custard, Yorkshire tea, and English cheese and biscuits. "I could've gone a bit off the wall and a bit crazy but I want people to actually enjoy what they're going to have," Willett said. "It's very much a menu of what I've liked and what I've had growing up."

Sergio Garcia
(2018)
Sergio celebrated winning his long-awaited maiden major in 2017 by returning to Augusta with a menu that had a bit of everything. Proceedings kicked off with a so-called "International Salad", which contained ingredients from countries of all Masters champions. The main course was arroz caldoso de bogavante, which is essentially Spanish lobster rice. Dessert was his mother's recipe for tres leches cake, served with ice cream.

Scottie Scheffler
(2023)
Texan star Scheffler laid on a four-course feast for his fellow Masters Club members when he returned to the scene of his major breakthrough in 2023. First on the menu were cheeseburger sliders – served 'Scottie Style' – alongside firecracker shrimp. Next up, was a tortilla soup, followed by one of two options for the main: a Texas ribeye steak or blackened redfish, served with macaroni and cheese, jalapeno creamed corn, fried brussels sprouts and fries. Dessert was a warm chocolate chip skillet cookie with 'milk and cookies' ice cream.

bunkered.co.uk

114 < bunkered.co.uk

THE **TASTES OF AUGUSTA**

The Tastes of Augusta

The Masters is more than a golf tournament. It's a feast for all the senses. In particular, the tastebuds...

WORDS **ALEX PERRY**

IN A SPORTING landscape that generally looks to squeeze every penny out of the consumer – particularly when it comes to being fed and watered – the Masters is, quite rightly, lauded around the world for its more-than-reasonable pricing. Not only that, the food is incredible too. Here are some of the standouts...

CHICKEN BISCUIT
Chicken? For breakfast? Only in America. And with biscuits? Well, not quite. Biscuit, in this context, is more like what we would know as a scone on this side of the Atlantic. But still, it's quite the epicurean experience.

PIMENTO CHEESE SANDWICH
The sandwiches are by far and away the headline act in this picturesque corner of Georgia. The $3 options include the formidable Pork Bar-B-Que, the Masters Club, and Ham and Cheese on Rye. But for just $1.50 – a little north of £1 in old money – you can get the famous Pimento Cheese. A mixture of cheese, mayonnaise and pimento, a small, sweet chilli, these are not for everyone. Though you have to try one. It's tradition, after all.

SOUTHERN CHEESE STRAWS
Crunchy, crumbly, cheesy. What's not to love here? The Masters-branded potato chips and peanuts are wonderful, but the Southern Cheese Straws are the pick of the savoury snacks at Augusta National.

GEORGIA PEACH ICE CREAM SANDWICH
If you have a sweet tooth, then there's plenty to cater for you, too, including Masters cookies, popcorn and moon pies. But you simply cannot go to Augusta and not try this. It comprises of two soft vanilla cookies packed with a slice of Georgia peach ice cream. It looks small when you first open it, but once you take that first bite you know you're in for a challenge. A delicate, delicious challenge.

CROW'S NEST BEER
And, of course, you need to wash it all down. All the usual soft drinks are on offer here at $2 a pop – get it? – and bottled water comes in at the same price. If you're partial to an alcoholic beverage, there's plenty of beer and wine on offer, costing $6 a glass, with the pick of the bunch being the Crow's Nest, a light, refreshing wheat ale brewed exclusively for the Masters and only available during tournament week.

AND ANOTHER THING...
Did you know you can buy Taste of the Masters hampers so you can enjoy Augusta's incredible culinary options from the comfort of your own home? The 'large hosting kit' features three huge tubs of Pimento Cheese, Pork Bar-B-Que and Egg Salad so you can make your own sandwiches, then a collection of sweet and savoury snacks and Masters branded cups and coasters. There is also a smaller 'classics kit'. Be quick, though, because they sell out fast!

bunkered.co.uk > 115

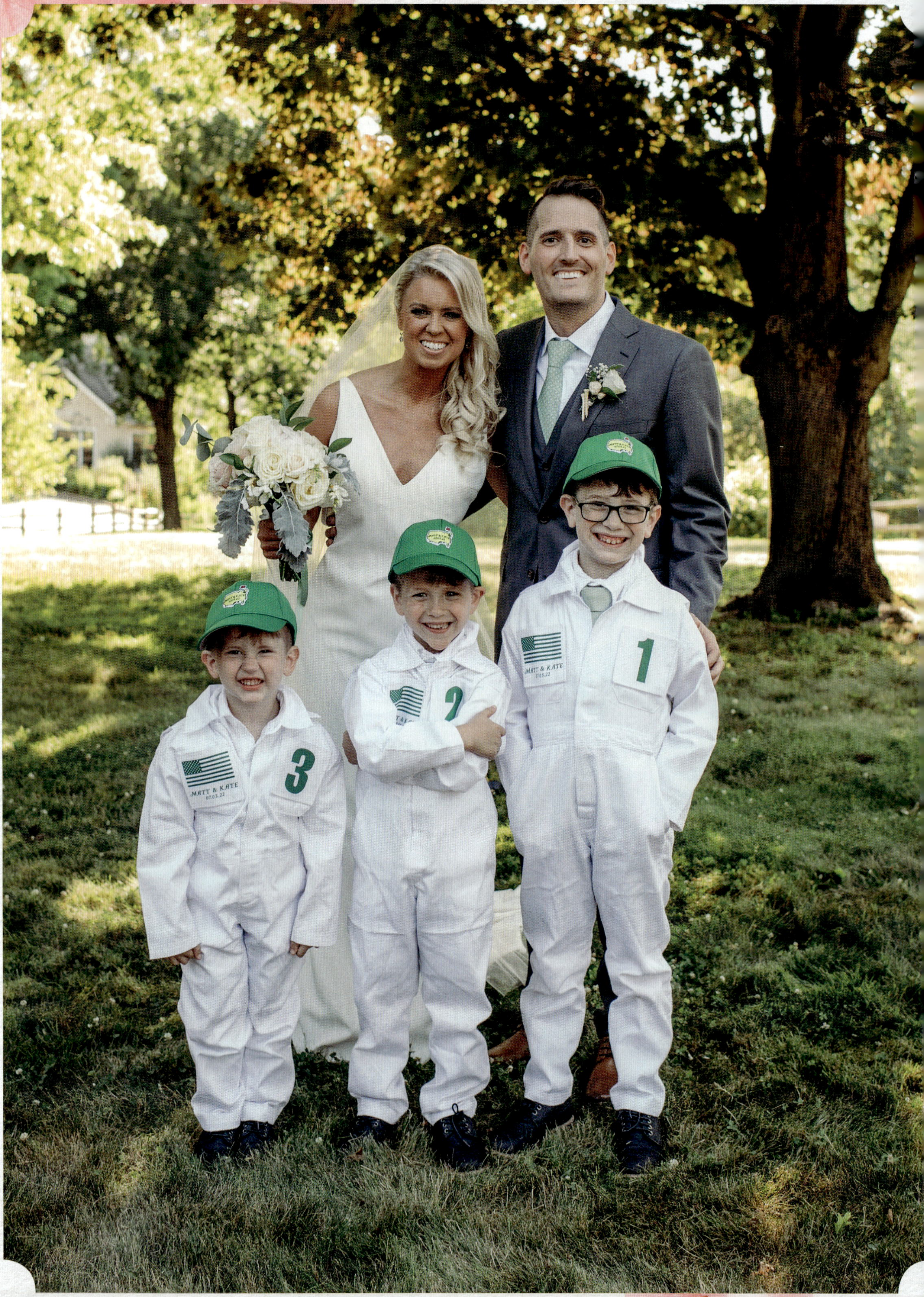
MATT & KATE
07.03.22
3
2
MATT & KATE
07.03.22
1

MASTERS **WEDDING**

A wedding *Unlike any Other*

So, you love the Masters, do you? You probably don't love it as much as Kate and Matt Ziance, a Connecticut couple who decided to incorporate the first men's major of the year into their wedding day... with stunning results.

WORDS **MICHAEL McEWAN** PHOTOGRAPHY **TAYLOR KEMP**

ASK ANYBODY WHO KNOWS and they'll tell you it's one of the greatest days of your life. A unique, one-of-a-kind experience, brimming with romance and sentiment, which completely exceeds your childhood dreams and has been known to make grown men cry. But enough about your first visit to the Masters. Weddings are fun, too. They're even more fun if you find a way to incoporate the first men's major of the season into them. That's what Matt and Kate Ziance did when they tied the knot on July 3, 2022. This is the fantastic inside story of their viral 'Masters Wedding'...

PENNSYLVANIA-BORN
Matt and Kate, from New Canaan, Connecticut, met through the dating app Hinge in the midst of the Covid-19 pandemic. As fate would have it, Kate was contemplating deleting the app from her phone while Matt was planning on moving back home to Johnstown. His lease on his Connecticut apartment was expiring and he had been placed on 'work from home' status for the foreseeable future. Nonetheless, with nothing to lose, they arranged to go on a date on June 6, 2020. After dropping Kate back at hers, Matt called his mum on his way back to his apartment. "Hey mum," he said. "I don't think I'm going to be moving back home after all."

Since then, the couple have spent nearly every day with each other and, on January 1, 2021, they moved in together.

One of the things they bonded over was golf. Matt describes himself as "an average adult golfer at best". He's has been playing for the last 22 years but only really started taking it seriously in the last five to six years.

Indeed, he was almost late for their first date because, of course, he had decided to slip out for a few holes.

"There's something about the game I just can't get enough of," he explains. "It was very clear from the beginning of our relationship that I spend a lot of time at the course, and Kate wanted to learn how to play so we could take on 18 together."

Never one to shirk a challenge, Kate signed up for a few lessons at the local public course and, within a few weeks, after plenty of late night range sessions, she was ready to hit the fairways. On October 10, 2021, they booked a same-day tee time at Oak Hills Park Golf Course in Norwalk. The third hole there is a 114-yard par-3. Kate grabbed her 7-iron, stepped up... and promptly holed-out for an ace. It was only her sixth ever round.

"If there was any doubt in my mind – and there wasn't – that day confirmed for me that Kate was my person and my golf-partner for life," Matt adds. Immediately, he began to make plans to ask Kate to marry him.

In April 2021, he went out to the shops to buy a new sleeve of golf balls. Instead, he returned a few hours later with an engagement ring.

"If you know me, you know that I'm terrible with keeping secrets and can't contain my excitement when gifts are involved," he laughs. "From middle school through college, I would always find Christmas and birthday presents, open them and then re-wrap.
It's even worse when I am giving gifts. I normally end up telling recipients about their Christmas presents around Halloween. I'm not a fan of waiting."

But wait he did. He decided to put off proposing until August 23, a special day for the Ziance family. His parents were married on that day in 1986. Matt himself was born on it in 1990. Finally, after an elaborate set-up that involved taking Kate on a fake work trip to Nashville, enlisting the support of country star Spencer Crandall and (naturally) playing a round of golf at the Hermitage Golf Club in Tennessee, Matt popped the question. Fortunately, Kate said yes.

"I went to Nashville with my girlfriend," Matt says, "and came back home with my fiancée." And that's when the fun truly began.

"I get asked all the time how I was able to convince my better-half to allow a Masters-inspired wedding and, truthfully, that's not the case at all," he adds. "This was 100% a joint decision.

"We initially considered going to Town Hall but agreed that if we had a ceremony and reception, that it would be a solid experience for everyone in attendance. We really wanted to personalise it, without any of the typical wedding day BS. We wanted a personalised ceremony, a great party for our closest friends and family and of course, our favorite thing: golf."

One of the first items on their agenda was creating a logo. They went through a

MASTERS WEDDING

few different versions before setting on their own take on the Augusta National Golf Club emblem.

Next up: music.

"Lucky for us, Kate and I live above the church we got married in and our congregation has Terry Flanagan, one of the best music directors around," Matt explains. "He discovered the sheet music for the Masters theme tune and played a wonderful rendition on the piano as I walked down the aisle with my parents."

As things started to take shape, the couple continued to find fun new ways to incorporate the Masters into their wedding. One of those was having 'Masters Caddies' play a part of the ceremony.

"This is where our niece and nephews enter the chat," Matt laughs. "The three boys, with 'ZIANCE' nameplates on their mini caddie uniforms, made sensational 'Ring Caddies' while our beautiful flower girl stole the show, scattering rose petals from a custom range bucket filled with balls and custom tees."

As the day drew closer, Matt had a wild idea and reached out to Jim Nantz, the long-standing and iconic host of Masters television coverage in the US. He explained their unique wedding plans and asked Nantz if he would be willing to send a video message for them to use to welcome their guests.

The next day, he opened his email inbox to find a reply from Nantz with a video 20-second video attached. As it began to play, Matt couldn't believe his eyes and ears.

"Hello, friends. It's Jim Nantz. I have the great honour of welcoming the newlyweds. Now, join me, let's put our hands together and welcome this wonderful couple, Kate and Matt Ziance. Have a lifetime of happiness." The video rolled as Matt and Kate entered the reception.

"My mind is still blown this happened," Matt says. "Having golf broadcasting royalty kick off our wedding was the perfect way to start the best night ever."

Following Nantz's intro, Matt was helped into a custom green jacket before the couple grabbed their putters and attempted to hole a lengthy putt along the wooden floorboards. "Did I miss the putt?" Matt says. "Sure did. But I won the day."

From custom 'Hello, friends' dinner menus to an illuminated neon sign, cornhole boards and bags, table-hole flags, a 'Green Jacket' seating chart, a golf flag guest book, a golf-themed tie and custom gear for the after-party, the Ziances made sure their reception was exactly what they wanted. They also had a cookie table – a Pennsylvania wedding tradition – which Matt's mum spent several months creating. "There were over 5,000 cookies in total," explains Matt. "Many of them were golf-themed and those that weren't had a 'Masters' card labelling each different style. It was amazing."

It all added up to a wedding unlike any other. All that remains now is for the couple to actually attend the Masters together.

"Yeah," Matt smiles. "That would be pretty sweet."

> **We really wanted to personalise it, without any of the typical wedding day BS. We wanted it to be 100% us.**

MASTERS **WEDDING**

122 < bunkered.co.uk

INSIDE THE **MASTERS SHOP**

Roll up, roll up!

The Masters is more than a golf experience. It's also a shopping experience – and an extremely lucrative one at that.

WORDS **MICHAEL McEWAN** PHOTOS **AUGUSTA NATIONAL/GETTY IMAGES**

SHOPPING HEAVEN
Clockwise from main: Patrons eye up purchases in the August National Golf Shop; the spectacular scene that awaits as you walk through the doors; a highly-prized Masters gnome.

WHAT'S THE ONLY thing better than going to the Masters? Simple: showing off to all of your friends that you've been to the Masters. And the best way to do that is with a bit (or several bits) of tournament-branded merchandise.

Welcome to the curious chaos of The Masters Golf Shop. Located between the driving range and the first fairway, the current shop opened in 2018 and cost around £35 million to build.

Twice the size of its predecessor, it is a hive of activity throughout the week of the tournament and for good reason. Unlike most other sporting events or franchises, Masters merchandise is only available to buy on-site. There's no online shop and no plans for one either. That makes the array of goods available both exceptionally sought-after and the ultimate golf humblebrag.

Slap a Masters logo on it and, quicker than you can say 'Mastercard', things that nobody will ever need inexplicably become things nobody can do without. And with more than 64 check-outs, there are no long queues to wait in, maximising the amount of time you can spend where it matters most: on the golf course.

Augusta National Golf Club doesn't publish how much money the shop brings in but it is reckoned to be in the region of $70 million each year. That's $10 million per day, $1 million per hour, $16,000 per minute, and $277 per second that the store is open.

It contains every kind of item you can imagine. There are close to 400 mannequins, showing off the various apparel options, with 125 different styles of hats on display.

There are also Masters-branded wristwatches, rucksacks, chopping boards, dog bowls, jigsaw puzzles, jute bags, candles laced with the 'Scent of Augusta', and so much more.

However, without question, the most keenly-anticipated item each year is the Masters gnome. Reportedly limited to just 1,000 per day, the garden ornaments were introduced in 2016 and feature a different design each year. One of the earliest had him decked out in the famous white caddie overalls. The 2024 version had the customary white beard, a navy cardigan and plaid trousers with a Masters golf bag slung over his shoulders.

If you want one, you need to be quick. If you're not across the shop threshold by 10am, you won't get one. It's that simple. For those lucky enough to get in there, there are two options to choose from: a full size one (around a foot high) priced at $49.50, or a smaller one, which comes in at just under $30.

As an example of just how in-demand the gnomes have become, you can expect to pay around $500 to get one (still boxed) from eBay, with a complete collection, from 2016 to now, conservatively estimated to be worth as much as $25,000.

Speaking of eBay, back in March 2024, when Augusta National gave patrons a first look at that year's design on social media, "Masters Garden Gnomes" were reportedly searched for more than 70 times per hour on the auction site. It is reckoned that the number of gnomes sold via eBay increased by 3,750% between 2016 and 2023.

An original 2016 gnome even sold for a record $2,250 on the auction site in 2023.

A shopping experience unlike any other? That is certainly one way of putting it.

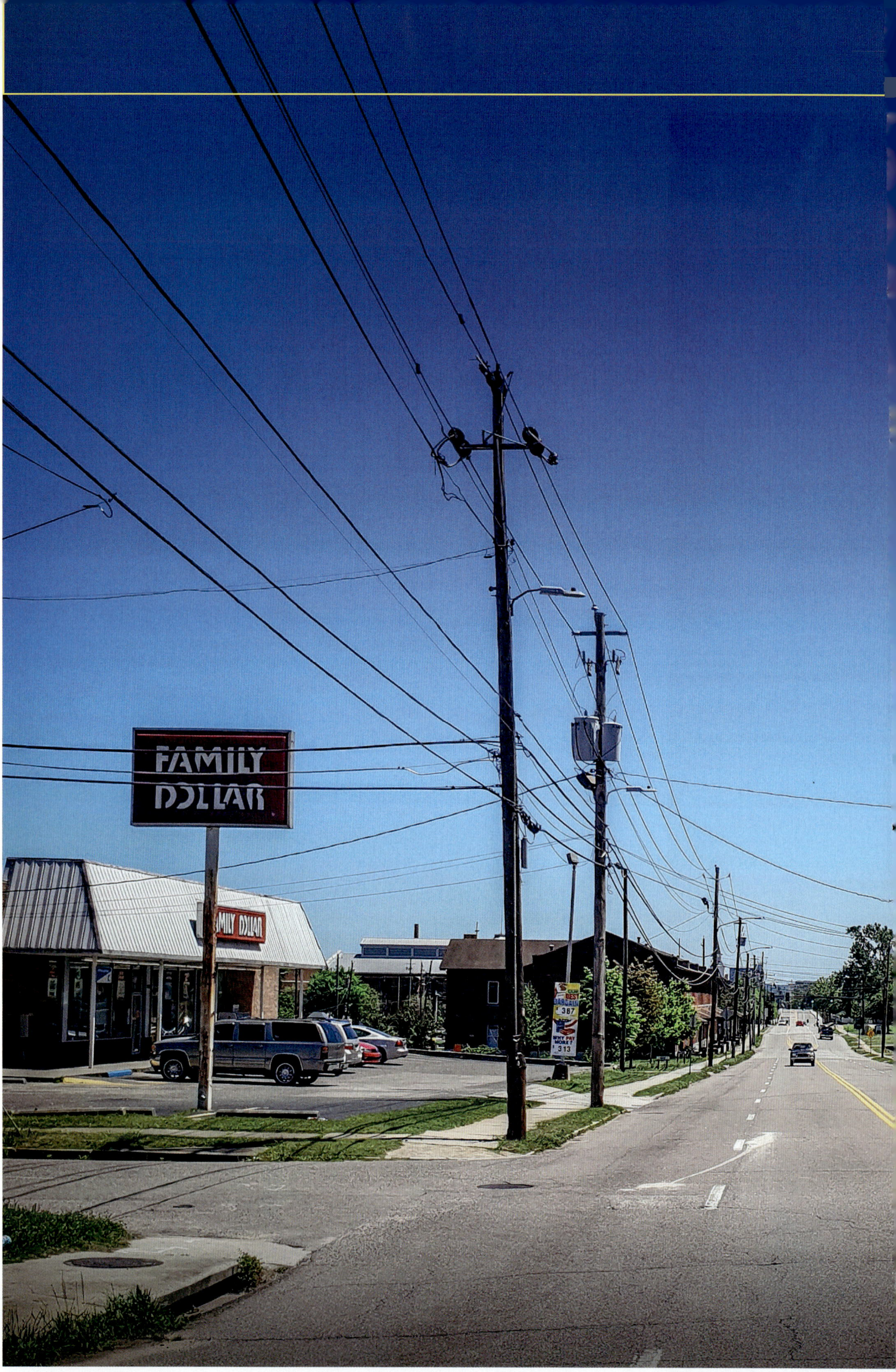
FAMILY
DOLLAR

THE AUGUSTA **YOU DON'T SEE**

DOWNTOWN

The Augusta *you* DON'T SEE

Michael McEwan goes for a walk around the Masters' home town and discovers it's not all azaleas and dogwoods.

PHOTOS **SUPPLIED / ADOBE STOCK**

MICHAEL EVERETT casts a glance at the empty car park outside the thrift store where he volunteers. "Where's yours?" he asks. I point 100 or so yards down the street to the Family Dollar convenience store. In the time it takes to blink, his face contorts into a concerned frown. "Hey, you gotta be careful," he insists. "This ain't your reg'lar neighbourhood. There are some crackerjacks round here, y'know? Maybe not so much today. It's colder today. But they out there. You gotta have your wits about you. 'Specially a guy like you. They'll know you ain't from 'round here."

It's the morning after the 2019 Masters Tournament and I'm on Broad Street, just three miles from Augusta National Golf Club. Three miles, but it might as well be three thousand. You don't find patrons down here. Poverty, yes. Patrons, no. The lawns are overgrown, the paint is peeling off the houses as though desperate to escape.

In this part of Augusta, the azaleas seldom bloom.

UP ON WASHINGTON ROAD, the television compound opposite the golf club is emptying fast. The mobile studios are rolling out and rolling away, taking their leave for another year. On the corner of Washington and Woodbine, the only evidence that a major golf tournament has just taken place is a huge billboard plastered with a Jordan Spieth advert for Rolex. It's hard not to wonder what's worth more: the Swiss timepieces or the houses adjacent.

Further down the street, the roadside ticket touts have gone from the front of the Dollar General, their week flipping the hottest tickets in town done for another 12 months.

Inside, shelves are being replenished. "This is always a crazy week for us," the cashier tells me. "We've sold out of loads of things: ice, deck chairs, hay fever tablets."

Even the 2D life-size cutout of Tiger Woods has gone from the front of the store. "All week, people stopped to get their picture taken with it," adds the server. "I don't know what happened to it. Maybe it got stolen, maybe somebody bought it. I don't know. All I know is it brought people in."

The gas station directly opposite the golf club has also enjoyed a profitable Masters. "It's like eight or nine times busier for us than a regular week," the clerk revealed. "It's good for the big guy in charge but doesn't change my pay cheque one bit. Just like any other week."

Washington Road is lined with just about every fast-food outlet you can think of. Arby's, McDonald's, Burger King, Chick-fil-A, Taco Bell, Bojangles, Five Guys, Red Lobster. This is the heartland of grab 'n' go America.

There's a Hooters, too. The perimeter fence surrounding it and marquee opposite it are coming down. For the umpteenth year, this particular restaurant has played home to John Daly, his family and their huge RV throughout Masters week. The two-time major winner last played in the first men's major of the season in 2006. Now, he uses the occasion as an opportunity to hawk signed merchandise to his legion of fans.

From 10am until 7pm each day, he, his partner Anna and various other members of Long John's entourage sell signed flags, signed caps, his distinctive Loudmouth clothing and much more besides from fold-down tables in front of their mobile home. It does a brisk trade, too. "We're busy all day, every day," says Anna. "This is my 11th year doing it. John's been doing it longer. It's great fun. John loves his fans." That love clearly doesn't extend to the media.

When I disclose that I'm a reporter from Scotland, he dives back inside his truck. Perhaps there's something that desperately needs his urgent attention on-board. Perhaps he's suspicious of reporters after a lifetime of media intrusion. Or perhaps he's embarrassed that, as the world's biggest golf tournament takes place no more than a mile up the road, he has been reduced to peddling his John Hancock for quick and easy cash.

On the other side of the golf club, the 'Mema Had One' antiques shop is dead. Unlike other shops on Washington Road, it has been all week. A shop-hand called Jimmy stops to talk. He's laden with an

THE AUGUSTA YOU DON'T SEE

HEADIN' DOWNTOWN
Clockwise from left: A dog stands guard at a house on Broad Street; an aerial view of Downtown Augusta; a typical back yard / junk yard off Broad Street.

bunkered.co.uk › 127

armful of branches but wants to chat. Jimmy seems like a nice guy, an elderly African-American with just two teeth, both on the bottom row. He points to a rusty old Chevy pick-up that sits in front of the shop and laughs. "Gimme an hour and I'll have her running for ya." He knows the Masters has just finished, knows that Tiger Woods has won. But, other than that, the tournament has largely passed them by. "Last year, we was busy one day. I think it rained that day. But don't nobody come down here. I don't know why. You'd think all them people being here that we'd be queued out to the street but we ain't. I don't know why. It's too bad."

Down on Broad Street, you get the sense that 'bad' would be an improvement.

TAKE A RIGHT TURN AT THE INTERSECTION OF BROAD STREET AND MILLEDGE ROAD – coming from Augusta National – and you'll arrive in Sand Hills and Summerville, two of the more prosperous parts of town. Houses here sell for north of $1 million. This is where you'll find Augusta Country Club, so too the Daniel Field airfield, the landing strip of choice for the private jets that shuttle the world's best golfers in and out for the Masters.

Go straight on at the Broad-Milledge intersection – on the opposite side of interstate 28 from Harrisburg – and you'll find a totally different way of life.

It's a community dear to the heart of Michael Everett. A tall black guy in his sixties, Everett is loud, animated and disarmingly gregarious. No sooner have I walked into the Mercy Ministries Thrift Store than he has rushed out from behind the counter to welcome me. "Come on in," he says, shaking my hand. "I hope you enjoy having a look around."

I can't help but notice he's wearing a Masters jumper, the little yellow logo giving the game away.

"Did you enjoy the final round yesterday?" I ask.

"Man, did you see that? Tiger Woods is BLACK! I mean, back," he says with a booming laugh. "Oh yes sir, Tiger Woods is BACK!"

You get the distinct impression that, without Everett, laughs would be hard to come by, both in this store – so disorganised and cluttered that it looks as though a tornado has ripped through it – and in the community. The abandoned house just down the street has a 'CONDEMNED' sign taped to its front door, sun-faded 'Paw Patrol' blinds in the front window all that remain of the kid or kids who once lived there. It's hard not to wonder what's become of them.

"People 'round here, they don't have much," Everett says. "That's why we do what we do. Come, let me show you."

He guides me into the annex, where black bin bags are piled ceiling high with clothes that have been donated. Beyond that is a dark, makeshift canteen where they serve food to locals who have either lost their homes or fallen on hard times. Through the adjacent door is a communal area, where volunteers are helping people with benefit applications, job applications, you name it.

Everett reckons they give away more than one hundred bags of food every month. Brand new $200 mattresses sell for $40. Clothes go for $10 a bag, kids' toys for less than a dollar. It's as far removed from the $4,000-a-year membership of Augusta National Golf Club as you can get. And yet it's no further from the front gates than a dozen of Rory McIlroy's very best drives.

I ask if Tiger winning would resonate with the community. "The thing about Tiger is when he plays, people come to town. You go up to Daniel Field and they all there. Michael Jordan's private jet is there. Condoleezza Rice's private jet is there. But when Tiger ain't here, they ain't here. And Tiger? Yeah, who ain't happy to see him back?

"Maybe it's even better because he's a brother. But you know what people 'round here would like? Just once? For Tiger to come down here, come to a black church. Just one time. Come and be with us. But he don't. He flies in to play and flies out to stay. I heard he stays in Atlanta when the Masters is on. I don't know that for sure but I believe it. It's too bad."

We talk some more and, as I leave, him showing me to door with a warning to be careful, he asks where I'm from.

"Lemme guess - Ireland?"
"Scotland, but close enough."
"You comin' back next year?"
"I hope so."
"You gonna come back to see me?"

I assure him I will but I know I'm lying.

He gives me a thumbs up and closes the door behind him.

Sitting on the street across the road, a man is having a furious argument with himself. A dog chained to the front porch of a house barks angrily as I walk past. Weeds grow through cracks in the ground and smother walls of ramshackle houses. I get in my car, lock the doors and drive away. As I hit interstate 20, bound for Atlanta airport, one word sits foremost in my mind.

Privilege.

Augusta juxtaposes both sides. The 'haves' of many inside the gates of Augusta National Golf Club, and the 'have nots' of many on the periphery.

The grass, as it turns out, is not always greener.

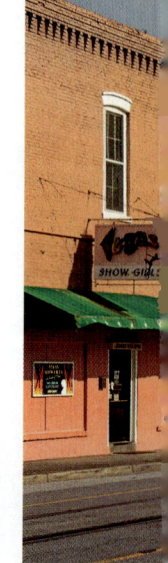

STREETS AHEAD
Colourful facades on the buildings on Sixth Street in Augusta.

THE AUGUSTA **YOU DON'T SEE**

TALKING SHOP
Left: A busted Chevy sits out front of the Mema Had One antiques store.
Below: Inside the Mercy Ministries Thrift Store.

THE ULTIMATE MASTERS QUIZ

So, you think you know everything there is to know about Augusta National? Let's see...

01 Which player has the most Masters victories with six?

02 Who was the first non-American player to win the Masters?

03 Who, at 21 years and 104 days old, holds the record for the youngest ever Masters champion?

04 Who is the only Scot to have won the Masters?

05 Nick Faldo turned a 54-hole six-shot deficit into a five-shot victory in 1996, but who did he overtake to clinch his third Green Jacket?

06 How many players have won the Par-3 Contest and the Masters in the same year?

07 Who was the last player to win the Masters at the first time of trying?

08 And which player needed a record 19 attempts to finally slip into the Green Jacket?

09 Who, in 1935, hit the first ever albatross at the Masters – later dubbed "the shot heard round the world" – to force a playoff before going on to win?

10 14-year-old Tianlang Guan was hit with a one-shot penalty in 2013, but for what?

11 Who was the first left-hander to win the Masters?

12 Greg Norman matched it in 1996, but which player, ten years earlier, was the first to card a round of 63 at the Masters?

13 I finished runner-up at the Masters a record four times without ever winning – who am I?

14 Who, at 69th, was the lowest-ranked player to win the Masters in the OWGR era?

15 Bob Goalby won the 1967 Masters after which player was disqualified for signing for an incorrect score?

16 There have only been three winning scores over par in Masters history: Sam Snead in 1954, Jack Burke in 1956, and which other player in this century?

17 Which legendary golfer is the only player to have lost a Masters playoff on more than one occasion?

18 Who is the only player to have finished runner-up in the Masters to both Jack Nicklaus and Tiger Woods?

ANSWERS 1. Jack Nicklaus. **2.** Gary Player. **3.** Tiger Woods. **4.** Sandy Lyle. **5.** Greg Norman. **6.** Zero. **7.** Fuzzy Zoeller. **8.** Sergio Garcia. **9.** Gene Sarazen. **10.** Slow play. **11.** Mike Weir. **12.** Nick Price. **13.** Tom Weiskopf. **14.** Angel Cabrera. **15.** Roberto De Vicenzo. **16.** Zach Johnson. **17.** Ben Hogan. **18.** Tom Kite.